Instructor-Student Handb

*to accompany*

# Counseling and Psychotherapy: Theories and Interventions

## Second Edition

David Capuzzi
Portland State University

Douglas R. Gross
Professor Emeritus
Arizona State University

Prepared by
Diane K. Unck
Portland State University

Merrill,
an imprint of Prentice Hall
*Upper Saddle River, New Jersey    Columbus, Ohio*

©1999 by Prentice-Hall, Inc.
Simon & Schuster/A Viacom Company
Upper Saddle River, New Jersey 07458

Printed in the United States of America

10 9 8 7 6 5 4 3 2 1

ISBN: 0-13-792938-2

# COUNSELING AND PSYCHOTHERAPY: THEORIES AND INTERVENTIONS

*David Capuzzi*
*Douglas R. Gross*

**Introduction and Overview**

**Acknowledgments**

**Suggestions for Use of the Instructor-Student Handbook**

---

**PART ONE: Foundations for Individual Counseling and Psychotherapy**

**PART TWO: Theories of Counseling and Psychotherapy**

**PART THREE: Integrative Theoretical Applications**

## INTRODUCTION AND OVERVIEW

This Instructor-Student Handbook has been designed to accompany the second edition of our text, <u>Counseling and Psychotherapy: Theories and Interventions</u> (Merrill/Prentice Hall, 1999). The major purpose of the handbook is to enhance both instruction and student learning in courses dealing with counseling and psychotherapy. An instructor-student format was selected since we view the learning process as being a partnership between the instructor and student. A partnership that provides not only for instructor generated learning approaches designed to impact both the class and the individual student, but also student generated learning approaches that are personalized to meet the specific needs of the individual student. This format provides for shared responsibility for learning. Both the instructor and the student are called upon to take responsibility for the learning that takes place and to work together to assure that both the instructional format and the individual learning are maximized to assure the most effective instruction/learning possible.

In designing the handbook, we asked our authors to put themselves in the place of both the instructor and the student and provide learning paradigms that they felt would meet the stated purpose of the handbook. In doing this, the following instructional-learning features are included for each of the eighteen chapters in the text:

1. **Pre-tests** to aid the individual student to measure his/her beginning knowledge of the information presented in each of the eighteen chapters.

2. **Chapter overviews** to provide both instructors and students a concise conceptualization of the major concepts included in each of the eighteen chapters.

3. A listing of **key terms** to aid both instructors and students in better understanding special terminology and concepts used in the chapter.

4. A listing of **key people** to assist both instructors and students to quickly identify the individuals who have played a major role in the development of specific aspects of the subject matter of the chapter.

5. **Classroom activities** designed for use by the instructor to enhance not only the experiential nature of the instruction but also to build groups and teams of individual students. Such groups and teams foster both student participation and

the enhancement of student responsibility for learning.

6.     **Individual activities** designed for use by the individual student in the classroom to enable the student to not only take responsibility for his/her learning but also to design learning experiences to better meet his/her specific and unique needs.

7.     A set of **questions for study and discussion** designed to assist both instructors and students to focus attention on the main concepts of the information presented in the chapter. Such questions are seen to aid both instructors and students to go above and beyond the material in the chapter and to realize the difficulty in arriving at definitive answers for many aspects of counseling and psychotherapy.

8.     **Suggested readings** are provided for the individual student to enable him/her to pursue, in greater depth more information in specific areas of personal interest.

9.     **Post-tests** to provide the individual student the opportunity to measure his/her comprehension of the material presented in the chapter, and, based on the accuracy of responses, to review areas needing further study.

## ACKNOWLEDGMENTS

As co-editors and authors of the "Instructor-Student Handbook," we would like to express appreciation to the many people who have made this handbook a reality. First, to the hundreds of students who have populated our classes and shared their ideas, energy, and constructive feedback regarding both didactic and experiential classroom and individual activities that are set forth for each of the chapters in the text. These activities have been tried, evaluated, and restructured to better meet the needs of not only the individual students but also the goals of the class as determined by the instructor. Second, to our colleagues in counselor education programs, both from our respective institutions and from across the country, who have been willing to share what they do and provided us with many creative approaches to teaching. Many of their ideas are incorporated in aspects of the "Instructor-Student Handbook." Third, to the 22 authors who have contributed chapters for this text and have gone beyond the context of the chapter to construct exciting and creative material for inclusion in the "Handbook."

Appreciation must also be extended to Diane Unck, research assistant, and Master's student in the rehabilitation counseling specialization in the counselor education program at Portland State University. Diane's expertise as a proofreader and formatter made this "Handbook" a reality.

## SUGGESTIONS FOR USE OF THE INSTRUCTOR-STUDENT HANDBOOK

As Counselor Educators, we are very aware of the time pressures that are placed on both instructors and students to not only deliver a large body of information but also, from a student's perspective, to assimilate this same information within the parameters of a semester, a term, a quarter, or an abbreviated summer session. Therefore, we have structured the Instructor-Student Handbook to aid instructors and students in both the delivery and assimilation of this large body of information. For the purpose of clarity, we have divided the suggestions that follow into "Suggestions for Instructors" and "Suggestions for Students."

For the purpose of brevity, suggestions made regarding a chapter or a specific aspect of the handbook, may have equal applicability across other chapters and other sections of the handbook. All suggestions are designed to maximize the combined use of both the textbook and the handbook. The suggestions that follow are based on the experience of both counselor educators and students who have successfully faced and effectively dealt with this challenge.

## SUGGESTIONS FOR INSTRUCTORS:

Before the class begins, review the entire **handbook** and become familiar with the type of material it contains. As an instructor, determine what will aid you the most in presenting the material and what fits best with your style of teaching. Before the class begins, review the **chapter overviews** as presented in the **handbook** to determine the most effective order of chapter presentation based upon your teaching style. You may wish to begin with the introductory chapter (Chapter 1) and then move to Chapter 5 which deals with research on the efficacy of group work. You may want to move from the introductory chapter to the discussion of ethics as applied to groups as presented in Chapter 7.

The **key terms** and **key people** section of the **handbook** can serve as a good introduction to each chapter. Prior to your presentation of the material in each chapter, ask students to define, explain, or discuss the terms, concepts, and people that appear on these lists. This could be handled as an assignment prior to beginning a chapter or as a regular procedure that will be used each time you begin a new chapter. It should aid the student by directing his/her attention to key points in the chapter and also enhance the student's responsibility in structuring his/her learning. It also stresses the partnership between instructor and student discussed previously.

The **classroom activities** section of the **handbook** can serve several purposes. First, each activity is designed around major tenets or concepts in each chapter. Therefore, you select to use those that will reinforce the points you deem most important for the students' learning. Second, each activity is experiential in nature and will aid you in adding balance between the didactic and experiential aspects of your course. Third, each activity forces student interaction with peers and fosters a sense of cohesiveness and connectedness. Fourth, each activity places responsibility on the students to share their experiences, knowledge, and skill not only with the other members of their group or team, but also with other members of the class. The fifth and final purpose centers on students taking greater responsibility for their own learning through their active participation as a group or team member.

The **individual activities** section of the **handbook** is designed mainly for the students but as the instructor you will not only need to encourage the students' pursuit of these activities, but also provide class time for them to report back in either oral or written form.

The **questions for study and discussion** section of the **handbook** is designed for use by either the entire class or individual students. As a class project, the questions could be used prior to or after the instructor's formal presentation of material for each chapter. They could also serve as the basis of oral or written reports conducted by either individual students or students operating as a group or team. Their use by the individual student will be explained in the **student section**.

As with the **individual activities** section of the **handbook**, the **suggested readings** section is designed mainly for the students but as the instructor you will need to encourage students to use this material and perhaps provide class time for reporting their findings.

## SUGGESTIONS FOR STUDENTS:

Prior to beginning the class, review the entire **handbook** and become familiar with the type of material it contains. Determine, based upon your learning style, the various sections of the **handbook** that will best meet your needs. Compare the **handbook** with the text. This should aid you in planning the most effective procedures for utilizing both volumes to enhance your individual learning style.

Prior to reading Chapter I, take and score the **pre-test**. This will not only provide you with a grasp of your knowledge of the material presented in Chapter I, but also it will give you an overview of what the author(s) feel are important concepts and facts in the chapter. This same procedure is recommended for all chapters in the textbook.

Having taken the **pre-test** for Chapter I, in reading the text, pay particular attention to the areas missed on the **pre-test**. This should aid you in focusing your study on areas needing greater attention. Review the questions answered incorrectly as you cover this same material in the chapter. This same procedure is recommended for all chapters in the textbook.

A review of the **chapter overview** and the listing of **key terms** and **key people**, prior to reading each chapter should aid you in understanding what the author(s) consider to be the major points and people in each chapter. Such information should enable you to organize your reading in such a way as to place emphasis on the major points highlighted by the author(s). This same procedure is recommended for all chapters in the textbook.

The **classroom activities** section of the **handbook** was designed to aid the instructor by providing him/her with ideas for adding experiential activities to the class. Review these activities and voice your opinion on those that you feel would be most beneficial to you based upon your learning style. These activities provide an opportunity for you to take a more active role in your education and voicing your opinion demonstrates your willingness to assume responsibility for your learning.

The **individual activities** section of the **handbook** was designed specifically for you, the individual student. These activities take you beyond the material covered in the text and provide you with an opportunity to actively seek information and experiences that best fit your needs and interests. The selection and successful completion of these activities demonstrate the degree of responsibility you are willing to take in structuring learning experiences to better fit your unique personal and professional needs.

The **questions for study and discussion** section of the **handbook** provides you with an opportunity to not only demonstrate your comprehension of the subject matter through oral or written response to the questions, but also directs your attention to areas that may need further investigation. Such further investigation will allow you to select those that have high interest for you and provide you the opportunity to demonstrate your investigative and research abilities as you attempt to find answers. Sharing your answers with the rest of the class will provide others with the benefit of your work and add depth to the information presented in the class.

The **suggested readings** section of the **handbook** was designed specifically for you, the student. The material included in this section goes above and beyond what is presented in the text and allows you to design learning experiences based upon your own needs and interests.

The **post-test** should be taken and scored following the completion of instruction for each chapter. Based upon both the instruction provided and your own review of the material, there should be a marked improvement in your score based upon a comparison with the **pre-test.** Areas still needing review should be obvious based upon your scoring of the **post-test**. If review of the material does not provide the desired answer, set up a meeting with the instructor to gain clarification.

# CHAPTER ONE
## HELPING RELATIONSHIPS IN COUNSELING AND PSYCHOTHERAPY

**CHAPTER PRE-INVENTORY**

**INSTRUCTIONS: PLEASE ANSWER THE FOLLOWING QUESTIONS BEFORE YOU READ THIS CHAPTER:**

✓ (T)  F    1. The **HELPING RELATIONSHIP** appears to be the cornerstone on which all effective helping rests.

✓ (T)  F    2. The **HELPING RELATIONSHIP** is a relationship that promotes the potential of all persons involved.

✓  T  (F)    3. The **HELPING RELATIONSHIP** is a relationship in which the needs of both client and counselor/therapist are equal.

✗  T  (F)    4. The **CORE OR BASIC CONDITIONS** relate directly to various personal characteristics or behaviors that the counselor/therapist brings to and incorporates into the helping relationship.

✓  T  (F)    5. **EMPATHIC UNDERSTANDING** is the ability of the counselor/therapist to feel for clients as opposed to feeling with clients.

✗ (T)  F    6. The counselor's/therapist's ability to enter the client's world is an example of **CONGRUENCE**.

✓ (T)  F    7. **RESPECT AND POSITIVE REGARD** are defined as the belief in the innate worth and potential of clients and the ability to communicate this belief.

✓ (T)  F    8. **GENUINENESS AND CONGRUENCE** describe the ability to be authentic in the helping relationship.

✓  T  (F)    9. **CONCRETENESS** is the ability on the part of the counselor/therapist to see the complete picture that clients paint with their words.

✓ (T)  F    10. **WARMTH** is the ability to communicate and demonstrate genuine caring and concern for clients.

✓  T  (F)    11. **IMMEDIACY** is the ability to deal with the past and present factors that operate within the helping relationship.

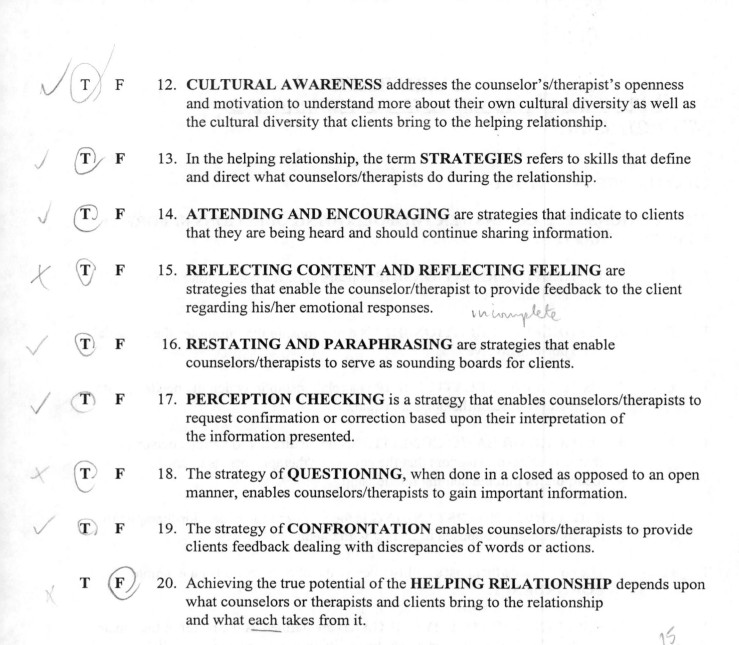

√ (T) F    12. **CULTURAL AWARENESS** addresses the counselor's/therapist's openness and motivation to understand more about their own cultural diversity as well as the cultural diversity that clients bring to the helping relationship.

√ (T) F    13. In the helping relationship, the term **STRATEGIES** refers to skills that define and direct what counselors/therapists do during the relationship.

√ (T) F    14. **ATTENDING AND ENCOURAGING** are strategies that indicate to clients that they are being heard and should continue sharing information.

✗ (T) F    15. **REFLECTING CONTENT AND REFLECTING FEELING** are strategies that enable the counselor/therapist to provide feedback to the client regarding his/her emotional responses.    *incomplete*

√ (T) F    16. **RESTATING AND PARAPHRASING** are strategies that enable counselors/therapists to serve as sounding boards for clients.

√ (T) F    17. **PERCEPTION CHECKING** is a strategy that enables counselors/therapists to request confirmation or correction based upon their interpretation of the information presented.

✗ (T) F    18. The strategy of **QUESTIONING**, when done in a closed as opposed to an open manner, enables counselors/therapists to gain important information.

√ (T) F    19. The strategy of **CONFRONTATION** enables counselors/therapists to provide clients feedback dealing with discrepancies of words or actions.

✗ T (F)    20. Achieving the true potential of the **HELPING RELATIONSHIP** depends upon what counselors or therapists and clients bring to the relationship and what each takes from it.

$\frac{15}{20}$

# CHAPTER 1 OUTLINE

**CHAPTER ONE**
**Helping Relationships in Counseling and Psychotherapy**

I.   **HELPING RELATIONSHIPS: DEFINITIONS AND DESCRIPTIONS**

II.  **HELPING RELATIONSHIPS: STAGES**

III. **HELPING RELATIONSHIPS:  CORE CONDITIONS**
  A.  Empathetic Understanding
  B.  Respect and Positive Regard
  C.  Genuineness and Congruence
  D.  Concreteness
  E.   Warmth
  F.  Immediacy
  G.  Cultural Awareness

V.   **HELPING RELATIONSHIPS: STRATEGIES**
  A.  Strategies That Build Rapport and Encourage Client Dialogue:
    1.  Attending and Encouraging
    2.  Restating and Paraphrasing
    3.  Reflecting Content and Reflecting Feeling
    4.  Clarifying and Perception Checking
    5.  Summarizing
  B.  Strategies That Aid in Data Gathering
    1.  Questioning
    2.  Probing and Leading
  C.  Strategies That Add depth and Enhance the Relationship
    1.  Self-Disclosure
    2.  Confrontation
    3.  Responding to Nonverbal Cues

VI:  **CONCLUSIONS**

VII: **REFERENCES**

## CHAPTER OVERVIEW

This chapter begins with a student scenario designed to set the stage for the presentation of various aspects of the helping relationship that serve as the foundation on which the process of counseling or psychotherapy rests. The first of these aspects is that dealing with definitions and descriptions of the parameters that surround the helping relationship. Building on these definitions and descriptions, the helping relationship is discussed in terms of four developmental stages that takes the helping relationship from its initial development through to termination and follow-up.

Another aspect of the helping relationship centers on the core or basic conditions that, when present, enhance the effectiveness of the relationship. These core or basic conditions include empathic understanding, respect and positive regard, genuineness and congruence, concreteness, warmth, immediacy, and cultural awareness.

Building on these core or basic conditions that need to be present for the effective development of the helping relationship, strategies are presented and refer to skills that define and direct what counselors or therapists do during the relationship to attain specific results and move the helping relationship from problem identification to problem resolution. These strategies are divided into three categories, strategies that build rapport and encourage client dialogue, strategies that aid in data gathering, and strategies that add depth and enhance the relationship.

The chapter concludes with a summary of the chapter content and reflections on the scenario that served as the introduction to the chapter.

## KEY TERMS

Helping Relationship
Stages
Relationship Development
Extended Exploration
Problem Resolution
Termination and Follow-up
Core/Basic Conditions
Empathic Understanding
Respect/Positive Regard
Genuineness/Congruence
Concreteness
Warmth
Immediacy
Cultural Awareness

Strategies
Attending and Encouraging
Restating and Paraphrasing
Reflecting Content
Reflecting Feeling
Clarifying
Perception Checking
Summarizing
Questioning
Probing
Leading
Self-disclosure
Confrontation
Nonverbal Responding

## KEY PEOPLE

A. Boy
L. Brammer
B. Barenson
R. Carkhuff
A. Combs
G. Corey
M. Corey
L. Cormier
W. Cormier
G. Egan

A. Ivey
B. Okun
S. Osipow
C. Patterson
G. Pine
C. Rogers
E. Shostrom
D. Sue
C. Truax
H. Hackney

## CLASSROOM EXERCISES TO ENHANCE INSTRUCTION AND STUDENT LEARNING

1. Divide the class into groups of three or four and instruct each group as follows:

   a. Each member of the group will play the following roles: (1) client, (2) counselor/therapist, and (3) observer. (NOTE: In groups of four, there will be two observers for each role-play.
   b. Have the group members select who will play which role for the first role-play.
   c. Instruct the person playing the **CLIENT** to role-play a client presenting for counseling for the first time. The problem presented is selected by the person playing the role.
   d. Begin the first session and let it run for 10 minutes. At the end of 10 minutes call time and ask the observers to give feedback.
   e. Repeat part "d" until all persons have had the opportunity to play all three roles.
   f. At the end of the role-play conduct a total group discussion focusing on the following:
      (1). As a counselor/therapist, what did you learn about your interaction with clients?
      (2). As a client, what did you learn about the feelings and behaviors that clients might demonstrate in the counseling relationship?
      (3). As observers, what did you learn about the counseling process?

2. Divide the class into four groups and assign each group one of the four helping relationship stages as outlined in the text. Ask each group to review the material dealing with the stage assigned and then demonstrate for the other members of the class what would take place in the assigned stage. Have each group emphasize the following:

   a. The goals and purposes of the stage.
   b. The role of the counselor/therapist.

c. The role of the client.

d. The relationship of this stage to the other three.

3.  Divide the class into seven groups and assign each group one of the seven core or basic conditions discussed in the text. Ask each group to review the material dealing with the core or basic conditions and have each group present the following information to the class:

   a. How the core or basic condition enhances the effectiveness of the helping relationship?

   b. How does the counselor/therapist develop the expertise to effectively use the core or basic condition?

   c. How does one measure the existence of the core or basic condition in the helping relationship?

   d. What behaviors or words are used to communicate the core or basic condition in the counseling session?

4. Conduct a demonstration of a first counseling session for the class. Select a volunteer from the class to serve as the client. Ask the client volunteer to construct a presenting problem. Conduct a 30 minute counseling session. Ask the class to observe and to pay special attention to the following:

   a. The presence or absence of core or basic conditions.

   b. The strategies used and their effectiveness.

   c. The stage(s) exemplified by the demonstration.

   After the demonstration, conduct a total class discussion encouraging honest feedback regarding the counseling process.

## INDIVIDUAL EXERCISES TO ENHANCE THE STUDENTS' LEARNING

1. Interview professional counselors/therapists and ask them the following questions:

   a. What do they see as the stage development of the counseling process?

   b. What do they see as the importance of the core or basic conditions and how do they measure their effectiveness?

   c. Which of the various strategies do they feel are most important in the counseling process?

   If time permits, share your findings with the rest of the class.

2. Based upon your specific area(s) of interest, i.e., children, adolescents, adults, the elderly, investigate, through library research and/or personal interviews, the similarities and differences that exist in the structure and content of the helping

relationship across these different age groupings.

If time permits, share your findings with the rest of the class.

3. Select another member of the class and ask him/her if he/she would be willing to do a videotape demonstration of a counseling session. Critique the session in terms of the existence and use of core and/or basic conditions and strategies. Select other members of the class to also critique the videotape demonstration.

If time permits, share your findings and the videotape with the rest of the class.

4. Based upon your specific area(s) of counseling interest, i.e., career, drugs/alcohol, eating disorders, depression, lifestyle issues, relationship issues, investigate, through library research and/or personal interviews, the similarities and differences that exist in the structure and content of the helping relationship in these specific counseling interest areas.

If time permits, share your findings with the rest of the class.

5. Check with your program and/or the audio-visual center on your campus and see if there are videos of counseling sessions. Ask two or more of your classmates to view the videotapes with you and critique in terms of the core or basic conditions and the strategies used in the counseling session.

If time permits, share your findings with the rest of the class.

## QUESTIONS FOR STUDY AND DISCUSSION

1. What do you see as the relationship between the various strategies identified in the text and the various theoretical systems also presented in the text?

2. How important is it for the counselor/therapist to have knowledge of the "stage development" process of the helping relationship? How would such knowledge enhance his/her ability to provide counseling/therapy?

3. If you accept the fact that the core or basic conditions discussed in the text are fundamental to the counseling/helping process, how does one incorporate these conditions into the ongoing process of counseling? Is it possible to teach the skills inherent in these core or basic conditions?

4. What do you see as the relationship between the various core or basic conditions identified in the text and the various theoretical systems also presented in the text? Do these core or basic conditions permeate all theoretical systems? If not, why not?

5. What relationship do you see between your own personality characteristics and the core or basic conditions presented in the text?  Are these core or basic conditions present or are these conditions you will need to learn?

## SUGGESTED READINGS

Benjamin, A. (1981).  *The helping interview*. (3rd. Ed.).  Boston:  Houghton Mifflin.

Brammer, L. M. & Shostrom, E. L. (1977).  *Therapeutic Psychology*.  (3rd. ed.). Englewood Cliffs, NJ:  Prentice-Hall.

Kottler, J. A. (1986).  *On being a therapist*.  San Francisco, CA: Jossey-Bass.

Kurpius, D.J. (1986).  The helping relationship.  In M. D. Lewis, R. L. Hayes, & J. A. Lewis (Eds.).  *The counseling profession* (pp. 96-129).  Itasca, IL:  Peacock.

Nugent, F.A. (1994).  *An introduction to the profession of counseling* (2nd. ed.). Englewood Cliffs, NJ: Merrill/Prentice Hall.

Pietrofesa, J.J., Hoffman, A., & Splete, H.H. (1984).  *Counseling:  An introduction* (2nd. ed.).  Boston:  Houghton Mifflin.

Watkins, C.E. Jr. (1990).  The effects of counselor self-disclosure:  A research review. *Counseling Psychologist*. 18, 477-500.

Young, M.E. (1992).  *Counseling methods and techniques*.  New York:  Macmillan.

**CHAPTER POST-INVENTORY**

**INSTRUCTIONS: PLEASE ANSWER THE FOLLOWING QUESTIONS NOW THAT YOU HAVE COMPLETED READING THIS CHAPTER.**

(T)  F  1. The **HELPING RELATIONSHIP** appears to be the cornerstone on which all effective helping rests.

(T)  F  2. The **HELPING RELATIONSHIP** is a relationship that promotes the potential of all persons involved.

T  (F)  3. The **HELPING RELATIONSHIP** is a relationship in which the needs of both client and counselor/therapist are equal.

(T)  F  4. The **CORE OR BASIC CONDITIONS** relate directly to various personal characteristics or behaviors that the counselor/therapist brings to and incorporates into the helping relationship.

T  (F)  5. **EMPATHIC UNDERSTANDING** is the ability of the counselor/therapist to feel for clients as opposed to feeling with clients.

T  (F)  6. The counselor's/therapist's ability to enter the client's world is an example of **CONGRUENCE**.

(T)  F  7. **RESPECT AND POSITIVE REGARD** are defined as the belief in the innate worth and potential of clients and the ability to communicate this belief.

(T)  F  8. **GENUINENESS AND CONGRUENCE** describe the ability to be authentic in the helping relationship.

T  (F)  9. **CONCRETENESS** is the ability on the part of the counselor/therapist to see the complete picture that clients paint with their words. *Incomplete*

(T)  F  10. **WARMTH** is the ability to communicate and demonstrate genuine caring and concern for clients.

T  (F)  11. **IMMEDIACY** is the ability to deal with the past and present factors that operate within the helping relationship.

(T)  F  12. **CULTURAL AWARENESS** addresses the counselor's/therapist's openness and motivation to understand more about their own cultural diversity as well as the cultural diversity that clients bring to the helping relationship.

(T)  F  13. In the helping relationship, the term **STRATEGIES** refers to skills that define and direct what counselors/therapists do during the relationship.

**(T)** F     14. **ATTENDING AND ENCOURAGING** are strategies that indicate to clients that they are being heard and should continue sharing information.

T **(F)**     15. **REFLECTING CONTENT AND REFLECTING FEELING** are strategies that enable the counselor/therapist to provide feedback to the client regarding his/her emotional responses.    *incomplete*

**(T)** F     16. **RESTATING AND PARAPHRASING** are strategies that enable counselors/therapists to serve as sounding boards for clients.

**(T)** F     17. **PERCEPTION CHECKING** is a strategy that enables counselors/therapists to request confirmation or correction based upon their interpretation of the information presented.

T **(F)**     18. The strategy of **QUESTIONING,** when done in a closed as opposed to an open manner, enable counselors/therapists to gain important information.

**(T)** F     19. The strategy of **CONFRONTATION** enables counselors/therapists to provide clients feedback dealing with discrepancies of words or actions.

**(T)** F     20. Achieving the true potential of the **HELPING RELATIONSHIP** depends upon what counselors or therapists and clients bring to the relationship and what each takes from it.

# CHAPTER TWO
## ACHIEVING A PERSONAL AND PROFESSIONAL IDENTITY

**CHAPTER PRE-INVENTORY**

**INSTRUCTIONS: PLEASE ANSWER THE FOLLOWING QUESTIONS BEFORE YOU READ THIS CHAPTER:**

T F 1. Graduate students enrolled in counselor education or psychology programs may be required to participate as **CLIENTS** in either **INDIVIDUAL OR GROUP COUNSELING.**

T F 2. Few educators and clinical supervisors are stressing the post degree expectation that **COUNSELORS** and **THERAPISTS** involve themselves in **COUNSELING** or **PSYCHOTHERAPY** and **CONSULTATION** to maintain **PERSONAL GROWTH, WELLNESS,** and **TREATMENT-PLANNING.**

T F 3. A continually increasing data base supports the concept that counselors and therapists are only effective if they are self-aware and able to use **THEMSELVES** as the instruments through which change occurs.

T F 4. Three commonly discussed models of health and wellness are: the **PERSONAL CHARACTERISTICS MODEL,** the **PSYCHOLOGICAL HEALTH MODEL,** and the **MULTIDIMENSIONAL MODEL.**

T F 5. Kinnier proposed **TEN CRITERIA** for psychological health.

T F 6. There has been a great deal of emphasis in the professional literature on **COUNSELOR WELLNESS BEHAVIORS.**

T F 7. The counselor's or therapist's **VALUES** are an **INTEGRAL** part of what is brought to a relationship with a client.

T F 8. **WILLIAMSON** believed that counselors and therapists could avoid letting clients know about their values.

T F 9. **C. GILBERT WRENN** was one of the first to suggest that practitioners were providing counseling and psychotherapy from a narrow cultural perspective.

T F 10. **BEHAVIORIST, COGNITIVE-BEHAVIORAL,** and **REALITY** theories emphasize utilitarian individualism.

T F 11. **CLAIRE HAMILTON USHER** provided some helpful guidelines for assessing the cultural bias inherent in theories of counseling and psychotherapy.

**T** F   12. When **CULTURAL ENCAPSULATION** occurs, assumptions and beliefs may not be questioned, and clients from diverse cultural backgrounds may not be treated effectively because of the operation of certain biases on the part of the professional.

**T** F   13. Counselors and therapists in settings that serve large numbers of seriously disturbed clients experience higher rates of **PERSONAL DEPLETION**.

T **F**   14. The ending of a helping relationship is never experienced as a **LOSS**.

**T** F   15. Not wanting to go to work may be a sign of **BURNOUT**.

T **F**   16. Viewing life as dull, heavy, or tedious may be a sign of **BURNOUT**.

**T** F   17. When four or more signs of burnout are evident, counselors or therapists have entered a **WARNING ZONE**.

T **F**   18. It is always necessary to enter counseling or therapy to achieve **PERSPECTIVE** and **BALANCE**.

**T** F   19. It is not possible to continue indefinitely as an effective counselor or therapist unless options for **RENEWAL** are considered and pursued.

T **F**   20. The health and wellness of the helper has much to do with the **ART FORM** inherent in the helping relationship.

**CHAPTER TWO**
**Achieving a Personal and Professional Identity**

I. **THE IMPORTANCE OF HEALTH AND WELLNESS**
    A. Approaches To Health and Wellness
        1. The Personal Characteristics Model
        2. The Psychological Health Model
        3. The Multidimensional Health and Wellness Model

II. **VALUES AND CULTURAL BIAS IN THEORY AND PRACTICE**
    A. Values In Theory and Practice
    B. Cultural Bias In Theory and Practice
        1. Assumptions About Normal Behavior
        2. Emphasis on Individualism
        3. Fragmentation By Academic Disciplines
        4. Dependence on Abstract Words
        5. Overemphasis on Independence
        6. Neglect of Client Support Systems
        7. Dependence on Linear Thinking
        8. Focus on Changing the Individual Rather Than the System
        9. Neglect of History
        10. Cultural Encapsulation

III. **THE DAILY WORLD OF THE PRACTITIONER**

IV. **ACHIEVING PERSPECTIVE AND BALANCE**
    A. Know the Warning Signs for Burnout
    B. Consider Networking Options
    C. Refer Clients When Appropriate
    D. Disengage From The Professional Role
    E. Consider Possible Options for Renewal

V. **THE IMPORTANCE OF A PERSONAL THEORY**

VI. **CONCLUSIONS**

VII. **REFERENCES**

## CHAPTER OVERVIEW

This chapter stresses the importance of achieving a personal and professional identity as the student begins the study of theories of counseling and psychotherapy and gains experience in translating theory into "practice." Personal and professional identity are interrelated and foundational to being able to understand, evaluate and apply the theories presented in the second section of the text. Since the health and wellness of the practitioner is a prerequisite to effectiveness, possibilities for addressing this topic are addressed through describing the personal characteristics, psychological health and multi-dimensional health and wellness models.

The values and cultural biases of each member of the helping professions impacts the use and application of theory as well as the structuring of the helping relationship. Readers of this chapter are encouraged to make personal assessments of both their values and sensitivity to culturally diverse populations. In addition, they are asked to evaluate the values and cultural biases upon which the theories presented in subsequent chapters are based.

This chapter also discusses the daily world of the practitioner and the importance of learning to cope with the stresses of professional demands. Finally, the importance of thinking about the conceptual frame of reference with which clients are approached is stressed. Readers are encouraged to think about their own traits and cultural experiences in the process of learning how to work effectively with clients.

## KEY TERMS

Personal identity
Professional identity
Assessment and treatment planning
Personal theory
Health and wellness
The personal characteristics model
Empathy
Client's frame of reference
Process-outcome research
Counselor/therapist affirmation
Positive regard
Love of others
The multidimensional health
and wellness model
Orthodox psychoanalytic point of view
Pro-choice
Gay/lesbian orientation
Internal locus of control
Cultural bias in theory and practice
Assumptions about normal behavior

Concreteness or specificity of
expression
Effective helpers
The psychological health model
Psychopathology
Self-actualization
Self-love
Self-knowledge
Self-confidence and self-control
A clear perception of reality
Courage and resilience
Balance and moderation
Holistic
Values in theory and practice
Value orientations
Euthanasia
External locus of control
Counselor/therapist neutrality
Cross-cultural
Emphasis on individualism

## KEY TERMS (con't)

Fragmentation by academic disciplines
Overemphasis on independence

Dependence on abstract words
Neglect of client support systems

## KEY PEOPLE

A. Adler
R. Carkhuff
G. Egan
S. Freud
K. Horney
C. Jung
R. Kinnier ✗ *Criteria for Psychological health*
J. Myers
P. Pedersen
(J. Samler) *Assisting Value is legit*
C. Truax
E. Williamson ✗ *open about Values*
*Kaslow* *Re Burnout*

G. Allport
A. Combs
E. Erikson
E. Fromm
M. Jahoda
E. Kelly
A. Maslow
C. Patterson *Values influence techniques*
C. Rogers
H. Sullivan
C. Vontress
✗ C. Wrenn *Counsellors providing from their Cultural Base*
*Usher* *Assess Cultural bias in theories*

*Christopher - moral visions*

## CLASSROOM EXERCISES TO ENHANCE INSTRUCTION AND STUDENT LEARNING

1. Divide the class into groups and have each group discuss one of the approaches to health and wellness. Have each group evaluate the strengths and weaknesses of the approach being discussed. Reconvene the total group to discuss the importance of maintaining a positive outlook on life while delivering service to clients.

2. The importance of maintaining awareness of one's own values and the ability to articulate how the values of the counselor or therapist affect work with clients cannot be underestimated. Divide the class into dyads and have each dyad discuss the following:

   a. Am I completely cognizant of my own values?
   b. Do my values influence my preference for particular theoretical frameworks (e.g., RET or Jungian concepts) and associated techniques and interventions?
   c. How will I resolve dilemmas that arise when my values and those of the client are oppositional?
   d. What is my belief about whether a professional can remain neutral and avoid communicating his or her value orientation?
   e. What is my role in helping clients more clearly delineate their values?

   *Value Neutral ?*
   *Delineate Values*

   After giving dyads an appropriate amount of time to engage in discussion focused upon the above questions, reconvene the group for discussion and debate relative to issues and questions that arose during discussions with a partner.

3. Organize a panel composed of students who represent different cultural, ethnic and racial groups.  Ask them to share their thoughts and feelings about the applicability of current theories of counseling and psychotherapy in cross and multi-cultural situations.  Encourage class interaction with panelists as the presentations of panel members are made.

## INDIVIDUAL EXERCISES TO ENHANCE STUDENTS' LEARNING

1. Discuss the importance of health and wellness to the role of the counselor or therapist.  What are some of the approaches to health and wellness which are commonly discussed in mental health circles?

2. How might the values and cultural biases of the chief proponent of a theory of counseling and psychotherapy influence the development of the theory?

3. Can a counselor or therapist avoid conveying his or her values to clients during the process of counseling and psychotherapy?

4. Discuss some of the cultural biases that exist in theoretical frameworks which are derivatives of Western culture.

5. How do you plan to cope with the demands of your role as a counselor or therapist in order to maintain a positive perspective?

## QUESTIONS FOR STUDY AND DISCUSSION

1. How could you use the contents of this chapter to evaluate your own health and wellness? After making such a personal assessment, outline the steps you will take to improve or maintain the level of health and wellness you believe to be essential for optimal functioning as a mental health professional.

2. Assess the experiences you have had in a cross cultural context. Do you think these experiences adequately prepared you for counseling diverse populations?  If the answer is "no", what steps do you plan to take to obtain the experience you need?

3. Do some additional reading on the topic of values and cultural bias in theory and practice.  Organize a study/discussion group on this topic.  After meeting for a number of sessions, ask your professor if you and your group could lead a discussion on the topic with the entire class.

4. Reread the section of the chapter on the "daily world of the practitioner".  What aspects of your role as a mental health professional do you feel will create the most stress? What do you plan to do to manage potential stressors?

5. List the eight warning signs for burnout; then, evaluate yourself with respect to each of these signs. What, if anything, do you need to do to maintain or improve your own sense of well being.

## SUGGESTED READINGS

Ardell, D. B. (1988). The history and future of the wellness movement. In J. P. Opatz (Ed), *Wellness promotion strategies: Selected proceedings of the eighth annual National Wellness Conference.* Dubuque, IA: Kendall/Hunt.

Christopher, J. C. (1996). Counseling's inescapable moral visions. *Journal of Counseling & Development*, 75, 17-25.

Coster, J. S., & Schwebel, M. (1997). Well-functioning in professional psychologists. *Professional Psychology: Research and Practice, 28, 5-13.*

Finch, E. S. & Krantz, S. R. (1991). Low burnout in a high-stress setting: A study of staff adaption at Fountain House. *Psychological Rehabilitation Journal*, 14, 15-26.

Hanna, F. J., & Bemak, F. (1997). The quest for identity in the counseling profession. *Counselor Education and Supervision*, 36, 194-206.

Mackey, R. A., & Mackey, E. F. (1994). Personal psychotherapy and the development of a professional self. *Families in Society: The Journal of Contemporary Human Services,* 75, 490-499.

Pedersen, P. (1987). Ten frequent assumptions of cultural bias in counseling. *Journal of Multicultural Counseling and Development, 15,* 16–22.

Schulz, R., Greenley, J. R. & Brown, R. (1995). Organization, management, and client effects on staff burnout. *Journal of Health and Social Behavior*, 36, 333-345.

Sue, S. (1997). Community mental health services to minority groups: Some optimism, some pessimism. *American Psychologist*, 32, 616-624.

Wrenn, C. G. (1962). The culturally encapsulated counselor. *Harvard Educational Review,* 32, 444–449.

# CHAPTER POST-INVENTORY

**INSTRUCTIONS: PLEASE ANSWER THE FOLLOWING QUESTIONS NOW THAT YOU HAVE COMPLETED READING THIS CHAPTER:**

**(T)** F     1. Graduate students enrolled in counselor education or psychology programs may be required to participate as **CLIENTS** in either **INDIVIDUAL OR GROUP COUNSELING.**

T **(F)**     2. Few educators and clinical supervisors are stressing the post degree expectation that **COUNSELORS** and **THERAPISTS** involve themselves in **COUNSELING** or **PSYCHOTHERAPY** and **CONSULTATION** to maintain **PERSONAL GROWTH, WELLNESS, AND TREATMENT-PLANNING.**

*No one mentioned a database*

T **(F)**     3. A continually increasing data base supports the concept that counselors and therapists are only effective if they are self-aware and able to use **THEMSELVES** as the instruments through which change occurs.

*Self Awareness allows the maturity to A and therefore become more effective.*

**(T)** F     4. Three commonly discussed models of health and wellness are: the **PERSONAL CHARACTERISTICS MODEL**, the **PSYCHOLOGICAL HEALTH MODEL**, and the **MULTIDIMENSIONAL MODEL.**

*9*    T **(F)**     5. Kinnier proposed **TEN CRITERIA** for psychological health.

T **(F)**     6. There has been a great deal of emphasis in the professional literature on **COUNSELOR WELLNESS BEHAVIORS.** *until very recently*

**(T)** F     7. The counselor's or therapist's **VALUES** are an **INTEGRAL** part of what is brought to a relationship with a client.

*Could not* T **(F)**     8. **WILLIAMSON** believed that counselors and therapists could avoid letting clients know about their values.

**(T)** F     9. **C. GILBERT WRENN** was one of the first to suggest that practitioners were providing counseling and psychotherapy from a narrow cultural perspective.

**(T)** F     10. **BEHAVIORIST, COGNITIVE-BEHAVIORAL,** and **REALITY** theories emphasize utilitarian individualism.

**(T)** F     11. **CLAIRE HAMILTON USHER** provided some helpful guidelines for assessing the cultural bias inherent in theories of counseling and psychotherapy.

**(T)** F  12. When **CULTURAL ENCAPSULATION** occurs, assumptions and beliefs may not be questioned, and clients from diverse cultural backgrounds may not be treated effectively because of the operation of certain biases on the part of the professional.

**(T)** F  13. Counselors and therapists in settings that serve large numbers of seriously disturbed clients experience higher rates of **PERSONAL DEPLETION**. *Stress*

T **(F)**  14. The ending of a helping relationship is never experienced as a **LOSS**.

**(T)** F  15. Not wanting to go to work may be a sign of **BURNOUT**. *Kaslow*

**(T)** F  16. Viewing life as dull, heavy or tedious may be a sign of **BURNOUT**.

T **(F)**  17. *2 or >* When four or more signs of burnout are evident, counselors or therapists have entered a **WARNING ZONE**.

T **(F)** ?  18. It is *always* necessary to enter counseling or therapy to achieve **PERSPECTIVE** and **BALANCE**.

**(T)** F  19. It is not possible to continue indefinitely as an effective counselor or therapist unless options for **RENEWAL** are considered and pursued.

**(T)** F  20. The health and wellness of the helper has much to do with the **ART FORM** inherent in the helping relationship.

*Not just expertise but the application of that expertise thro' well being inspiration goes to perfect the art form*

# NOTES

1ª 5 Limitations on Code of Ethics –

# CHAPTER THREE
## _ETHICAL AND LEGAL ISSUES IN COUNSELING AND PSYCHOTHERAPY_

**CHAPTER PRE-INVENTORY**

**INSTRUCTIONS:  PLEASE ANSWER THE FOLLOWING QUESTIONS BEFORE YOU READ THIS CHAPTER:**

**T**   F   1. As an area of inquiry, **ETHICS** is a branch of philosophy that focuses on morals and morality as they relate to decision making.

**T**   F   2. **CODES OF ETHICS** regulate the behavior of members of the profession.

**T**   F   3. One **LIMITATION** of codes of ethics is their lack of adequate coverage for certain areas within the codes.

T   **F**   4. According to Kitchener, the term NONMALEFICENCE means causing harm to others.

**T**   F   5. According to Kitchener, the term **BENEFICENCE** means contributing to the welfare of the client.

**T**   F   6. **MEMBER RESPONSIBILITY** is central to all ethical behavior.

**T**   F   7. The term **MEMBER COMPETENCE** centers on the providing of only those services and techniques for which the member is qualified by training or experience.

**T**   F   _No_  8. **MEMBER COMPETENCE** is one of the areas in the codes of ethics that has been clearly defined.

**T**   F   _No_  9. The concept of **MEMBER COMPETENCE** is generally viewed from an external frame of reference.   _S/N/B ✓  s/B both._

**T**   F   10. **CLIENT WELFARE** serves as the focal point around which all codes of ethics revolve.

**T**   F   11. **CLIENT ACCESSIBILITY** refers to the client's ability to choose to participate in therapy.

T   **F**   12. The terms **CONFIDENTIALITY**  and  **PRIVILEGED COMMUNICATION** mean the same thing.

T (F) ? 13. The term **CONFIDENTIALITY** is limited to the verbal communication between the therapist and clients.

(T) F 14. **DUAL RELATIONSHIPS** have reference to the member's involvement with clients in a capacity other than that of a professional helper.

T (F) 15. Both codes of ethics advise counselors and psychologists not to engage in sexual intimacies with former clients/patients for at least 5 years after the termination of the professional relationship. 2

(T) F 16. The **MANAGED CARE INDUSTRY** presents possible ethical dilemmas for many counselors and therapists.

(T) (F) 17. When clients have difficulty availing themselves of counseling/therapeutic services due to issues of race, ethnicity, religion, gender, etc., this is referred to as **DUE CARE.** Counsellor issue        Access

(T) F 18. It is best for counselors/therapists to tell clients at the beginning of the helping relationship that **CONFIDENTIALITY** does not exist in certain situations.

on part of Counsellor
(T) F 19. **DUE CARE** refers to not placing clients in compromising situations that will either detract from the treatment or cause physical or psychological harm.

(T) F 20. The term **CONFIDENTIALITY** is best viewed as a client right.

# CHAPTER 3 OUTLINE

**CHAPTER THREE**
**Ethical and Legal Issues in Counseling and Psychotherapy**

I.    **ETHICAL CODES: DEFINITIONS AND RATIONALE**

II.   **MODELS OF ETHICAL DECISION MAKING**
     A.  Kitchener's Model for Ethical Decision Making  *5 :*
     B.  Forester-Miller and Davis Model  *7 steps*
     C.  Capuzzi-Gross Model

III.  **DIMENSIONS OF ETHICAL BEHAVIOR**
     A.  Member Responsibility
     B.  Member Competence
     C.  Member-Client Relationships
          1.  Freedom of Choice
          2.  Client Accessibility
          3.  Confidentiality
          4.  Informed Consent
          5.  Dual Relationships
          6.  Sexual Involvement
          7.  Other Professional Relationships
          8.  Technology
     D.  Other Issues

IV.   **DIMENSIONS OF UNETHICAL BEHAVIOR**

V.    **PROCESSING OF COMPLAINTS OF UNETHICAL BEHAVIOR**

VI.   **LEGAL ISSUES**
     A.  Duty to Warn
     B.  Due Care

VII.  **CONCLUSIONS**

VIII. **REFERENCES**

## CHAPTER OVERVIEW

Determining what is or is not ethical behavior often creates a perplexing dilemma for both the novice and the experienced practitioner. While the helping professions have offered practitioners a plethora of guidelines and codes of ethical behavior, confusion still exists.

To aid the reader in dealing with this confusion, the authors present information dealing with definitions and rationales of ethical codes, limitations of ethical codes, three models of ethical decision making, dimensions of ethical behavior including discussions of member responsibility, member competency, and member-client relationships. Each of these areas identifies not only the ethical privileges that apply but also situations to alert the practitioner to the possible existence of ethical dilemmas in these areas. This section concludes with a brief discussion of the possible ethical dilemmas generated by the rapidly developing entity entitled managed care.

Dimensions of unethical behavior drawn from the annual reports of professional ethics committees are also reported together with a general outline of the procedures utilized in the processing of complaints of unethical behaviors.

The last section of the chapter deals with legal issues in counseling and therapy with special attention paid to duty to warn and due care. The chapter concludes with suggestions for dealing with the complex issues that are central to ethical decision making.

## KEY TERMS

Ethics
Codes of ethics
Standards
Guidelines
Certification
Licensure
Managed Care
Ethical violations
Morals
Morality
Values
Ethical Behavior
Member
Malpractice
Ethical decision making
Nonmaleficence

Member competence
Member-client relationship
Freedom of choice
Client welfare
Client accessibility
Confidentiality
Informed consent
Dual relationships
Sexual involvement
Other professional relationships
Technology
Duty to warn
Due care
Adjudication
Autonomy
Beneficence

## KEY TERMS (con't)

Justice                              Fidelity
Ethical dilemma                      Client welfare
Legal Issues                         Member responsibility

## KEY PEOPLE

B. Anderson                          L. Swenson
P. Arredondo                         R. True
D. Brown                             W. Van Hoose
P. Calanan                           V. Vetter
B. Calfee                            J. Chauvin
G. Corey                             M. Corey
T. Davis                             L. Everstine
D. Everstine                         H. Forester-Miller
D. Frey                              W. Gibson
G. Heymann                           F. Ibrahim
H. Johnson                           K. Kitchner
J. Kottler                           K. Pope
T. Remley                            S. Robinson
R. L. Schwitzgebel                   R. K. Schwitzgebel
R. Seiden                            D. Srebelus

## CLASSROOM EXERCISES TO ENHANCE INSTRUCTION AND STUDENT LEARNING

1. Divide the class into small groups and present each group with the following "ethical situation" Have each group review the "ethical situation" and reach consensus on the following questions:

    a. What is the ethical issue(s) involved in the situation?
    b. What should the counselor/therapist do in the situation?

### *Ethical Situation*

The counselor/therapist has been working with the client for the past month. Just recently, the client announces that he/she has AIDS. Based upon the knowledge that the counselor/therapist has gained from the client, the counselor/therapist knows that the client remains sexually active. When asked, the client says that he/she does not tell his/her sexual partners and does not plan to do so for fear of rejection. The session ends and the counselor/therapist spends a good deal of time attempting to decide what he/she should do. After each group responds to the questions, conduct a total class discussion about the "ethical situation."

2. Divide the class into small groups and ask each group to review the ACA <u>Code of Ethics and Standards of Practice</u> (1995) and the APA <u>Ethical Principles of Psychologists and Code of Conduct</u> (1992). Have each group discuss the following questions:

   a. What are the similarities and differences between the two documents?
   b. Which document seems to provide the most comprehensive view of ethical procedures and why?

   Have each group report back to the total group and then conduct a total class discussion of the various responses.

3. Place the five moral principles of Kitchener (1984) on the board (**AUTONOMY, NONMALEFICENCE, BENEFICENCE, JUSTICE, FIDELITY**). Ask students to write their position on the five principles as it relates to their role as a counselor/ therapist. After the students have had an opportunity to complete this activity, place them in groups of three or four and ask them to share their positions. Prior to assembling the total group, have each group address the following question:

   a. Based upon your position on the five moral principles, what impact will this have not only on your approach to counseling and therapy but also what impact does this have to your behaving ethically?

   Have each group report back to the total group and then conduct a total class discussion of the various responses.

4. Divide the class into groups of five or six and ask each group to address the following:

   a. You are a member of either the American Counseling Association or the American Psychological Association and you have been asked to serve on the Ethics Committee. Your first task is to review and revise the existing models for ethical decision making. Using the three models presented in the text, select one and describe how you would add to, delete from, or reconfigure the model. Provide a rationale for your decisions.

   Each group is asked to report back to the total group.

5. Conduct a mock licensing or credentialing board hearing in class. To carry this out you will need to do the following approximately two weeks prior to the mock hearing:

   a. Develop a claimant's statement charging unethical behavior. (Assign this to a group in class)
   b. Develop the counselor's/therapist's written response to the charges. (Assign this to a group in class. This group will need the claimant's statement prior to

developing its response)

   c. Assign roles for claimant, counselor/therapist, and 5 or 6 members of the licensing/credentialing board. All persons involved in the mock hearing need to read the developed statements prior to the hearing.

   d. Conduct the hearing. After the hearing conduct a total class discussion.

## INDIVIDUAL EXERCISES TO ENHANCE STUDENTS' LEARNING

1. Interview practicing counselors and therapists and attempt to find answers to the following questions:

   a. How do you determine when ethical issues are involved with your interactions with clients?

   b. What procedures do you use in ethical decision making?

   c. What advice do you have for a person just entering the profession regarding the role ethics will play in his/her work with clients?

Request time to share your findings with the rest of the class. This could be done either through a written or oral report.

2. Interview a member of your state licensing or certification board and attempt to get answers to the following questions: (Note: if your state does not have licensing or certification for counselors talk with the licensing board for psychologists)

   a. What types of ethical complaints are most frequently filed against counselors/therapists in this state?

   b. What is the makeup of the licensing/certification board? How are board members selected? What is your meeting schedule?

   c. What do you see as the major problem(s) the board faces in attempting to police its professional members?

Request time to share your findings with the rest of the class. This could be done either through a written or oral report.

3. In order to better understand the differences between the ethical issues related to individual versus multiple-client involvement, compare and contrast either the ACA Code of Ethics and Standards of Practice (1995) or the APA Ethical Standards of Psychologists and Code of Conduct (1992) with either the AAMFT Code of Ethics (1991) or the Ethical Code for the International Association for Marriage and Family Counselors (1993).

Request time to share your findings with the rest of the class. This could be done either through a written or oral report.

4. Interview an attorney who specializes in mental health adjudication. Attempt to get answers to the following questions:

   a. What state/national laws or statutes have special application to counseling and therapy?
   b. What suggestions do you have for a person new to the field to become better informed as to the legal ramifications of counseling and therapy?

   Request time to share your findings with the rest of the class. This could be done either through a written or oral report.

5. Develop an ethical situation that deals with one of the areas mentioned in the text and give the situation to two or more practicing counselors or therapists. Have each person respond to the following:

   a. What, if any, are the ethical dilemmas in the situation?
   b. If there are ethical dilemmas in the situation, how would you resolve the situation?

   Request time to share your findings with the rest of the class. This could be done either through a written or oral report.

## QUESTIONS FOR STUDY AND DISCUSSION

1. Based on the fact that codes of ethics are designed to have application to the role and function of professional members as counselors and therapists, what specific guidelines are presented to provide direction to the counselor/therapist as consultant, supervisor, researcher, employee?

2. If you were asked to restructure and/or rewrite either the American Counseling Association's or the American Psychological Association's Code of Ethics, what would you add, delete or reconfigure? What would be your rationale?

3. Assume that you are a member of both the American Counseling Association and the American Psychological Association and that, as such you are called upon to uphold both codes. What areas within these two codes are conflictual to you as a member of both groups? In what areas will you find general agreement?

4. If you were asked to redesign the models of ethical decision making presented in the text, what would you add, delete or reconfigure? What is your rationale?

5. Considering the impact that managed care companies have and will continue to have on the broad field of mental health, what steps would you take to make the relation-ship between the counselor/therapist and managed care companies more compatible?

What steps would you take to assure client rights and still remain within the demands and constraints of managed care?


## SUGGESTED READINGS

Anderson, D., & Swanson, C. (1991). *Legal issues in licensure.* Alexandria, VA: American Counseling Association.

Butler, K. (1994). Duty of care. *Family Therapy Networker*, 18, 10-11.

Costa, L., & Altekruse, M. (1994). Duty-to-warn guidelines for mental health counselors. *Journal of Counseling and Development*, 72, 346-350.

Crawford, R.L. (1994). *Avoiding counselor malpractice.* Alexandria, VA: American Counseling Association.

Davis, T., & Richie, M. (1993). Confidentiality and the school counselor: A challenge for the 1990s. *School Counselor.* 41, 23-30.

Harding, A.K., Gray, L.A., & Neal, M. (1993). Confidentiality limits with clients who have HIV: A review of ethical and legal guidelines and professional policies. *Journal of Counseling and Development*, 71, 297-304.

St. Germaine, J. (1993). Dual relationships: What's wrong with them? *American Counselor,* 2, 25-30.

Thomas, V. (1994). Value analysis: A model of personal and professional ethics in marriage and family counseling. *Counseling and Values*, 38, 193-203.

Thompson, A. (1990). *Guide to ethical practice in psychotherapy.* New York: Wiley.

Woody, R.H. (1988). *Fifty ways to avoid malpractice.* Sarasota, Fl: Professional Resource Exchange.

## CHAPTER POST-INVENTORY

**INSTRUCTIONS: PLEASE ANSWER THE FOLLOWING QUESTIONS NOW THAT YOU HAVE COMPLETED READING THIS CHAPTER:**

**T**  F  1. As an area of inquiry, **ETHICS** is a branch of philosophy that focuses on morals and morality as they relate to decision making.

**T**  F  2. **CODES OF ETHICS** regulate the behavior of members of the profession.

**T**  F  3. One **LIMITATION** of codes of ethics is their lack of adequate coverage for certain areas within the codes.

T  **F**  4. According to Kitchener, the term **NONMALEFICENCE** means causing harm to others.

**T**  F  5. According to Kitchener, the term **BENEFICENCE** means contributing to the welfare of the client.

**T**  F  6. **MEMBER RESPONSIBILITY** is central to all ethical behavior.

**T**  F  7. The term **MEMBER COMPETENCE** centers on the providing of only those services and techniques for which the member is qualified by training or experience.

T  **F**  8. **MEMBER COMPETENCE** is one of the areas in the codes of ethics that has been clearly defined.

T  **F**  9. The concept of **MEMBER COMPETENCE** is generally viewed from an external frame of reference.

**T**  F  10. **CLIENT WELFARE** serves as the focal point around which all codes of ethics revolve.

*false* **T**  F *?*  11. **CLIENT ACCESSIBILITY** refers to the client's ability to choose to participate in therapy.

T  **F**  12. The terms **CONFIDENTIALITY** and **PRIVILEGED COMMUNICATION** mean the same thing.

T  **F**  13. The term **CONFIDENTIALITY** is limited to the verbal communication between the therapist and clients.

**T**  F  14. **DUAL RELATIONSHIPS** have reference to the member's involvement with clients in a capacity other than that of a professional helper.

T **(F)** 15. Both codes of ethics advise counselors and psychologists not to engage in sexual intimacies with former clients/patients for at least 5 years after the termination of the professional relationship.

**(T)** F 16. The **MANAGED CARE INDUSTRY** presents possible ethical dilemmas for many counselors and therapists.

T **(F)** 17. When clients have difficulty availing themselves of counseling/therapeutic services due to issues of race, ethnicity, religion, gender, etc., this is referred to as **DUE CARE.**

**(T)** F 18. It is best for counselors/therapists to tell clients at the beginning of the helping relationship that **CONFIDENTIALITY** does not exist in certain situations.

**(T)** F 19. **DUE CARE** refers to not placing clients in compromising situations that will either detract from the treatment or cause physical or psychological harm.

**(T)** F 20. The term **CONFIDENTIALITY** is best viewed as a client right.

# NOTES

42

# CHAPTER FOUR
## *PSYCHOANALYTIC THEORY*

**CHAPTER PRE-INVENTORY**

**INSTRUCTIONS:  PLEASE ANSWER THE FOLLOWING QUESTIONS BEFORE YOU READ THIS CHAPTER:**

**T**   F   1.  The **SECOND HISTORICAL PERIOD** of the psychoanalytic movement was dominated by the establishment of the American Psychoanalytic Association.

**T**   F   2.  According to Freud, **MENTAL ACTIVITY**  is not meaningless or accidental, nothing happens by chance or in a random way.

X   **T**   F  –   *Reaction Formation*   3.  **REPRESSION** is a process whereby an individual takes the opposite stance to protect self from awareness of his/her gratification in an abhorred position.

**T**   F   4.  In psychoanalytic theory, **PSYCHOSEXUAL STAGES** refer to sequential acquisition of progressively sophisticated modes of gratification from various bodily zones that are necessary for growth and development.

**T**   F   5.  The term **LIBIDO** describes instinctual energy that belongs to the sexual drive.

X  –   T   **F**   6.  According to Erikson, **ORALITY** represents a method of relating to the external world.

T   **F**  –   7.  The **OEDIPUS COMPLEX** dominates the **ANAL** stage of  human development.

**T**   F   8.  According to the information presented in the text, there are four distinct psychoanalytic psychologies within psychoanalysis.  These are **DRIVE THEORY, EGO PSYCHOLOGY, OBJECT RELATIONS PSYCHOLOGY** and **SELF PSYCHOLOGY.**

**T**   F   ?   9.  The assumptions upon which the system of psychoanalytic theory rests are referred to as **METAPSYCHOLOGY**

**T**   F   10.   The **TOPOGRAPHIC** view, in psychoanalytic theory, contrasts unconscious versus conscious mental processes.

T  (F)   11. The **GENETIC** point of view, in psychoanalytic theory, refers to the origin and development of psychic phenomena.

T  (F)   12. The **ID, EGO**, and **SUPEREGO** are examples of the **DYNAMIC** and **ECO-NOMIC** point of view in psychoanalytic theory.

T  (F)   13. The term "**RULE OF ABSTINENCE**" is a term used to describe a client's behavior in counseling or therapy.

(T)  F   14. In psychoanalysis, **TRANSFERENCE** is the client's reliving in the presence of the counselor or therapist his/her repetitious and rigid defenses of the past.

(T)  F   15. In psychoanalysis, the most important analytic procedure is **INTERPRETATION** - making an unconscious phenomena conscious.

(T)  F   16. **PSYCHOANALYSIS** in the United States has traditionally been limited to the educated, middle to-upper class client who is able to afford the cost of treatment.

X   (T)  F   17. In psychoanalytic clinical work, it is not essential to have the client's association to a dream in order to verify our assumptions about the **LATENT** unconscious meaning of a **SYMBOL** or the dream itself.

(T)  F   18. In psychoanalytic theory, the metapsychological construct of **ADAPTATION** deals with a person's relationship to his or her environment.

X   T  (F)   19. In psychoanalysis, **EMPATHY, INTUITION**, and the counselor's/therapist's own unconscious and theoretical knowledge all contribute to the construction of an interpretation.

(T)  F   20. One of the **LIMITATIONS** of psychoanalysis is that the urban and rural poor, as well as the rural middle and upper class, have not had access to psychoanalytic services.

16/20

**CHAPTER 4 OUTLINE**

**CHAPTER FOUR**
**Psychoanalytic Theory**

I.   **BACKGROUND**

II.  **HUMAN NATURE:  A DEVELOPMENTAL PERSPECTIVE**
    A.  The Freudian Unconscious
    B.  Freud's Developmental Theory
    C.  Post-Freudian Psychoanalytic Theory

III. **MAJOR CONSTRUCTS AND THE PROCESS OF CHANGE**

IV.  **APPLICATIONS**
    A.  Overview
    B.  Goals of Counseling and Psychotherapy
    C.  Intervention Strategies

V.   **EVALUATION**
    A.  Overview
    B.  Supporting Research
    C.  Limitations

VI.  **THE CASE OF MARIA:  THE PSYCHOANALYTIC APPROACH**

VII. **REFERENCES**

## CHAPTER OVERVIEW

This chapter provides a brief outline of both psychoanalytic theory and counseling and therapy techniques. Background information focuses on the early work of Sigmund Freud and presents the development of psychoanalysis from the turn of the century to the present. Emphasis is placed on the three historical periods of psychoanalysis encompassing time periods from the late 1800s through World War I (Stage I); between World War I and World War II (Stage II); and post World War II (Stage III).

The Freudian unconscious, Freud's theory of development and the expansions and extensions of Freud's original work serve as content for a discussion of the human development perspective of psychanalysis. This discussion covers both Freud's early work plus current extensions of psychoanalysis such as ego psychology, self psychology, and object relations psychology.

The major constructs of psychoanalysis are explained in terms of metapsychology and the six points of view that are necessary to comprehend a psychic event thoroughly. These views encompass the topographic, dynamic, economic, genetic, structural, and adaptive.

The goals of psychoanalytic theory are presented and the intervention strategies of free association, dream analysis, analysis of transference, analysis of resistance, and interpretation are discussed in relationship to the case of Maria.

The evaluation section aids the reader in better understanding the place research has played and continues to play in the ongoing development and use of psychoanalysis as a treatment modality. The limitations of psychoanalysis concludes this section of the chapter.

The case of Maria serves as a central theme in aiding the reader to comprehend the application of psychoanalytic theory as the authors analyze the case from a psychoanalytic perspective. The chapter concludes with a summary.

## KEY TERMS

Displacement
Condensation
Psychosexual stages
Defense mechanisms
Repression
Drive Theory
Ego Psychology
Object Relations Psychology
Self-Psychology
Supportive Therapy

Erogenous Zone
Oedipus Complex
Intersubjective Theory
Relational Theorizing
Social Constructivism
Countertransference
Metapsychology
Topographic
Dynamic
Economic

## KEY TERMS (con't)

Reeducative Therapy

Reconstructive Therapy

Psychic Determinism

Id

Ego

Superego

Hypothesis

Secondary Process

Regression

Repression

Reaction Formation

Undoing

Introjection

Genetic

Structural

Adaptive

Pleasure Pain Principle

Constancy Principle

Tension-discharge

Primary Process

Rule of Abstinence

Transference

Interpretation

Isolation

Projection

## KEY PEOPLE

C. Brenner

A. Freud

W. Fairbain

P. Giovacchini

H. Kohut

H. Rabin

E. Erickson

S. Freud

R. Fine

R. Greenson

F. Pine

L. Wolberg

## CLASSROOM EXERCISES TO ENHANCE INSTRUCTION AND STUDENT LEARNING

1. Distribute a listing of the defense mechanisms to all students and explain how defense mechanisms fit into the psychoanalytic process. Answer questions students may have about the defense mechanisms. After you feel students understand the defense mechanism, ask students to do the following:

   a. Have each student identify the various defense mechanisms he/she uses and identify a situation in his/her life that exemplifies the use of the defense mechanism and the purpose it serves.
   b. Move through the defense mechanisms and provide an opportunity for students to share their use, situations, and purposes with other members of the class. Conduct a total group discussion of the defense mechanisms.

2. Invite a psychoanalytic counselor/therapist to speak to your class. Ask him/her to address the following:

a.  The theoretical basis of psychoanalysis
b.  His/her training background
c.  Intervention strategies
d.  Current approaches
e.  Limitations of the theory in application

Allow time for a question and answer period following the presentation.

3.  Divide the class into four groups and ask each group to research one of the four different approaches to psychoanalytic psychology (Drive Theory, Ego Psychology, Self-Psychology, Object Relations Psychology).  Stress that each group should report on the following:

a.  Major constructs of the approach
b.  Similarities and differences from the other three approaches
c.  Intervention strategies
d.  Types of cases where this approach is most effective

Have each group present its findings to the total group.

4.  Have students report a dream and discuss in a group, encouraging students to free associate to their dreams during the discussion.

5.  Have two volunteers role-play a 10 to 15 minute counseling session (made-up problem) and have rest of students make notes on defense mechanisms used, possible conflicts in the problem, and the nature of the experience between client and counselor.  Conduct a class discussion of the experience.

## INDIVIDUAL EXERCISES TO ENHANCE STUDENTS' LEARNING

1.  Interview a counselor/therapist who identifies himself/herself as psychoanalytic in orientation.  In the course of the interview, you might want to ask the following:

a.  What do you see as the strengths of this theoretical orientation?  Are there special types of presenting problems that are most effectively treated with this theoretical orientation?
b.  What do you see as the limitations of this theoretical orientation?  Are there special types of presenting problems that would not be most effectively treated with this theoretical orientation?
c.  What direction might you give someone like myself who is attempting to develop knowledge and expertise in the area of theories applicable to counseling and therapy?

Ask the instructor for time to present your findings, either in written or oral form to members of your class.

2. If you are a person who dreams and is able to recall your dreams, keep a journal of your dreams. If you are comfortable with sharing your dream journal, ask a class member to work with you on interpreting your dreams. Based again on your comfort level, ask the instructor for time to present your findings, either in written or oral form to members of your class.

3. Using either the reference citations found at the end of the chapter or the suggested readings in this handbook, write a brief paper comparing Freud's "Drive Theory" with one of the newer extensions of this theory (Ego Psychology, Self-Psychology, Object Relations Psychology).

   Ask your instructor for time to share your findings, either in written form or orally, with the other members of your class.

4. Research the artist Jackson Pollock (or one of the Surrealists) whose work purported to visually depict the unconscious.

5. Present a paper/discussion on a book or movie that depicts a central theme in psychoanalysis. For example the movie Remains of the Day as an example of sexual repression, or Shakespeare's Oedipus Rex as an "acting out" of the conflicts in the Oedipal Complex.


## QUESTIONS FOR DISCUSSION

1. What place do you see the psychoanalytic approach having in what the authors refer to as "the development and proliferation of a variety of abbreviated psychotherapeutic strategies or convenience market approaches" to mental health?

2. In psychoanalysis what is the relationship between the terms "unconscious mental processes" and "psychic determinism"?

3. What is meant by Greenson when he states, "The clinical implications of metapsychology intimate that in order to comprehend a psychic event thoroughly, it is necessary to analyze it from six different points of view - the topographic, dynamic, economic, genetic, structural, and adaptive"?

4. The psychoanalytic approach sets forth various psychosexual stages of development. Where do you find agreement and disagreement with this stage typology?

5. Based upon the limitations of psychoanalytic practice cited by the authors, what do you see as ways of removing these as limitations?

## SUGGESTED READINGS

Erikson, E.H. (1982). *The life cycle completed.* New York: Norton.

Freud, S. (1923/1933). *New introductory lectures on psychoanalysis.* New York: Norton.

Freud, S. (1923/1947). *The ego and the id.* London: Hogarth Press.

Freud, S. (1900/1955). *The interpretation of dreams.* London: Hogarth Press.

Hall, C.S. (1954). *A primer of Freudian psychology.* New York: The American Library.

Jones, E. (1953). *The life and work of Sigmund Freud.* (Vol.1). New York: Basic Books

Jones, E. (1955). *The life and work of Sigmund Freud.* (Vol. 2). New York: Basic Books.

Jones, E. (1957). *The life and work of Sigmund Freud.* (Vol. 3). New York: Basic Books.

Kohut, H. (1971). *The analysis of self.* New York: International Universities Press.

Kohut, H. (1984). *How does psychoanalysis cure?* Chicago: University of Chicago Press.

Leak, G.K., & Christopher, S.B. (1982). Freudian psychoanalysis and sociobiology. *American Psychologist*, 37, 313-322.

Winkler, K. J. (1986). Scholars prescribe Freud's "talking cure" for problems. *Chronicle of Higher Education*, 33(8), 4-6.

## CHAPTER POST-INVENTORY

**INSTRUCTIONS: PLEASE ANSWER THE FOLLOWING QUESTIONS NOW THAT YOU HAVE COMPLETED READING THIS CHAPTER.**

T   F     1.  The **SECOND HISTORICAL PERIOD** of the psychoanalytic movement was dominated by the establishment of the American Psychoanalytic Association.

T   F     2.  According to Freud, **MENTAL ACTIVITY** is not meaningless or accidental, nothing happens by chance or in a random way.

T   F     3.  **REPRESSION** is a process whereby an individual takes the opposite stance to protect self from awareness of his/her gratification in an abhorred position.

T   F     4.  In psychoanalytic theory, **PSYCHOSEXUAL STAGES** refer to sequential acquisition of progressively sophisticated modes of gratification from various bodily zones that are necessary for growth and development.

T   F     5.  The term **LIBIDO** describes instinctual energy that belongs to the sexual drive.

T   F     6.  According to Erikson, **ORALITY** represents a method of relating to the external world.

T   F     7.  The **OEDIPUS COMPLEX** dominates the **ANAL** stage of human development.

T   F     8.  According to the information presented in the text, there are four distinct psychoanalytic psychologies within psychoanalysis. These are **DRIVE THEORY, EGO PSYCHOLOGY, OBJECT RELATIONS PSYCHOLOGY** and **SELF PSYCHOLOGY.**

T   F     9.  The assumptions upon which the system of psychoanalytic theory rests are referred to as **METAPSYCHOLOGY**

T   F   10.  The **TOPOGRAPHIC** view, in psychoanalytic theory, contrasts unconscious versus conscious mental processes.

T   F   11.  The **GENETIC** point of view, in psychoanalytic theory, refers to the origin and development of psychic phenomena.

T   F   12.  The **ID, EGO,** and **SUPEREGO** are examples of the **DYNAMIC** and **ECONOMIC** point of view in psychoanalytic theory.

T   F   13.  The term **"RULE OF ABSTINENCE"** is a term used to describe a client's behavior in counseling or therapy.

**T  F**     14. In psychoanalysis, **TRANSFERENCE** is the client's reliving in the presence of the counselor or therapist his/her repetitious and rigid defenses of the past.

**T  F**     15. In psychoanalysis, the most important analytic procedure is **INTERPRETATION** - making an unconscious phenomena conscious.

**T  F**     16. **PSYCHOANALYSIS** in the United States has traditionally been limited to the educated, middle to-upper class client who is able to afford the cost of treatment.

**T  F**     17. In psychoanalytic clinical work, it is not essential to have the client's association to a dream in order to verify our assumptions about the **LATENT** unconscious meaning of a **SYMBOL** or the dream itself.

**T  F**     18. In psychoanalytic theory, the metapsychological construct of **ADAPTATION** deals with a person's relationship to his or her environment.

**T  F**     19. In psychoanalysis, **EMPATHY, INTUITION,** and the counselor's/therapist's own unconscious and theoretical knowledge all contribute to the construction of an interpretation.

**T  F**     20. One of the **LIMITATIONS** of psychoanalysis is that the urban and rural poor, as well as the rural middle and upper class, have not had access to psychoanalytic services.

# CHAPTER FIVE
## JUNGIAN ANALYTICAL THEORY

**CHAPTER PRE-INVENTORY**

**INSTRUCTIONS: PLEASE ANSWER THE FOLLOWING QUESTIONS BEFORE YOU READ THIS CHAPTER:**

T     F     1. **CARL GUSTAV JUNG** was a cohort of Sigmund Freud.

T     F     2. An accredited **JUNGIAN TRAINED COUNSELOR** or psychotherapist must undergo intense personal analysis.

T     F     3. **JUNG'S THEORIES** grew out of his personal background and familial relationships.

T     F     4. The **COMPLEX** and **ARCHETYPE** are interchangeable.

T     F     5. **SYMBOLS** are alive with meaning.

T     F     6. The **PSYCHE** is only a portion of all psychic processes.

T     F     7. **DREAMS** show the reality of the **PSYCHE**.

T     F     8. **EGO** is the center of the field of the unconscious.

T     F     9. The **RELIGIOUS INSTINCT** emanates from the **SELF**.

T     F     10. **PSYCHIC ENERGY** or **LIBIDO** is found in the conscious mind.

T     F     11. There are two **FUNCTIONS** and four **ATTITUDES** making up eight typology combinations.

T     F     12. **DREAMS** only reflect day residues.

T     F     13. **DREAMS** compensate conscious life.

T     F     14. Working with the **TRANSFERENCE** is integral to Jungian oriented counseling and psychotherapy.

T    F        15. Fairy tales reveal the **ARCHETYPAL** process of individuation.

T    F        16. Myth **MOTIFS** are an aspect of each person's psyche.

T    F        17. The **EGO** is the regulator of the personality.

T    F        18. Each person has an **ANIMA** and **ANIMUS**.

T    F        19. The **SHADOW** has personal and collective aspects.

T    F        20. When the **PERSONA** is rigid, the **ANIMA** and **ANIMUS** are poorly formed.

# CHAPTER 5 OUTLINE

**CHAPTER FIVE**
**Jungian Analytical Theory**

I. **BACKGROUND**

II. **HUMAN NATURE: A DEVELOPMENTAL PERSPECTIVE**
   A. Ego
   B. Persona
   C. Shadow
   D. Anima
   E. Animus
   F. Self

III. **MAJOR CONSTRUCTS**
   A. Psychological Types
   B. Complex
   C. Archetype
   D. Symbol
   E. Collective Unconscious

IV. **APPLICATIONS**
   A. Overview
   B. Goals of Counseling and Psychotherapy
   C. The Process of Change
   D. Intervention Strategies
      1. Dreams
      2. Transference and Countertransference
      3. Active Imagination

V. **EVALUATION**
   A. Overview
   B. Supporting Research
   C. Limitations

VI. **THE CASE OF MARIA: A JUNGIAN APPROACH**

VII. **REFERENCES**

## CHAPTER OVERVIEW

Jungian counseling or psychotherapy uses the presenting symptoms as material to lead into the deeper layers of the psyche. The complexes, archetypes, and symbols help each person realize her/his place in humanity and connection to others while working through the psychological conflicts.

Although Jungian work appreciates the second half of life for development, understanding early childhood issues is integral to the treatment. The blending of personal with collective, spiritual with physical matter, masculine and feminine, and all of the numerous paradoxes in life are part of the process of personality integration. Developing the capacity for internal communication comes from gaining familiarity with the various aspects of the personality - discovered through dreams, active imagination, daily life, synchronistic events, and the therapeutic process.

The individual who looks within finds the treasures gleaned from the process learned in this form of treatment. The discovery of oneself unfolds throughout a lifetime.

## KEY TERMS

Collective Unconscious
Spirit
Ego
Dream
Complex
Shadow
Projection
Animus
Compensatory
Amplification
Archetype
Personal Unconscious
Typology

Self-Regulation
Attitude
Psyche
Soul
Instinct
Symbol
Persona
Anima
Active Imagination
Function
Individuation
Libido
Participation Mystique

## KEY PEOPLE

Carl Gustav Jung

# CLASSROOM EXERCISES TO ENHANCE INSTRUCTION AND STUDENT LEARNING

1. Divide the class into small groups with each group analyzing the same dream. Amplify the symbols and identify the predominant complex and treatment issues. Comment on the ego, persona, anima, animus, shadow, and self aspects appearing in the dream.

   After each group has had an opportunity to complete the assigned task, have each group report back to the total group. Conduct a class discussion of the exercise. Allow time for questions and answers.

2. Divide the class into groups that describe the various components of a "mother complex" and a "father complex" and have each group list mythological and archetypal associations.

   After each group has an opportunity to complete the assigned task, have each group report back to the total group. Conduct a class discussion of the exercise. Allow time for questions and answers.

3. Ask for two students to volunteer and conduct a role-playing session demonstrating the techniques of transference and countertransference.

   After the demonstration, conduct a class discussion of the methods specific to Jungian counseling and psychotherapy. Allow time for questions and answers.

4. Divide the class into small groups and analyze a fairy tale using the major constructs of Jungian analytical psychology. Each group is to identify the major character or ego position, the masculine and feminine components, psychological issues, the problems presented, the shadow characters, the self symbols, and the process of psychological union.

   After each group has an opportunity to complete the assigned task, have each group report back to the total group. Conduct a class discussion of the exercise. Allow time for questions and answers.

5. Invite a Jungian analyst to speak to the class. Ask her/him to address issues dealing with theory and practice. Allow time for a question and answer period.


# INDIVIDUAL EXERCISES TO ENHANCE STUDENTS' LEARNING

1. Keep a dream journal for the length of the course including amplifications and emotional reactions to dreams. Include in your journal comments about personal learning from the experience. If you are comfortable, ask the instructor for time to

share your experiences with the rest of the class in either written or oral report form.

2. Examine and write a commentary on your favorite fairy tale as a metaphor for your life journey. Use the major constructs of Jungian Analytical Psychology and identify the major character or ego position, the masculine and feminine components, psychological issues, the problems presented, the shadow characters, the self symbols, and the process of psychological union.

   If you are comfortable, ask the instructor for time to share your experience with the rest of the class in either written or oral report form.

3. Take the Myers-Briggs Test and analyze the results in terms of the personality typology of Jung. Ask one or two other members of the class to join you in this activity. Compare and contrast your results with the impressions of the other members of your group.

   If you are comfortable, ask the instructor for time to share your experience with the rest of the class in either written or oral report form.

4. Interview a Jungian analyst in your community or at your university. Structure the interview so that you gain answers to questions dealing with both theory and practice. Ask the instructor for time to share your findings with the rest of the class in either written or oral report form.

5. Identify five of your favorite symbols and amplify their meanings as they have implications for your life and life tasks.

   If you are comfortable, ask the instructor for time to share your experience with the rest of the class in either written or oral report form.

## QUESTIONS FOR STUDY AND DISCUSSION

1. As you review the concepts of Jungian Analytical Psychology, how do you see these differing from other theoretical orientations? How are they alike? What in Jungian Analytical Psychology appeals to you? What does not appeal to you?

2. As you review the methods used by the Jungian counselor or psychotherapist to provide therapy, how do you see these differing from those of other theoretical approaches? How are they alike? What appeals to you most about the methods? What does not appeal to you?

3. What did Jung mean by the concept "psyche" and what parts do the "personal" and "collective unconscious" play in this concept?

4. What is the significance of the term "persona" in Jungian psychology and how does this relate to the concepts of "ego", "shadow", and "anima and animus"?

5. How does Jung operationalize the statement, "Dreams are the most natural way to discover and unravel the inner workings of the personality?

## SUGGESTED READINGS

Edinger, E. (1990). *The living psyche: A Jungian Analysis in Pictures.* Wilmette, IL: Chiron.

Engelsman, J. (1994). *The feminine dimension of the divine.* Wilmette, IL: Chiron Publications.

Hanna, B. (1981). *Active imagination as developed by C.G. Jung.* Santa Monica, CA: Sigo Press.

Henderson, J. (1990). *Shadow and self: Selected papers in Analytical Psychology.* Wilmette, IL: Chiron Publications.

Hillman, J. (1996). *The soul's code.* New York: Random House.

Homans, P. (1995). *Jung in context.* Chicago, IL: University of Chicago Press.

Hubback, J. (1988). *People who do things to each other.* Wilmette, IL: Chiron Publications.

Kast, V. (1990). *The creative leap: Psychological transformation through crisis.* Wilmette, IL: Chiron Publications.

Meier, C.A. (1989). *Healing dream and ritual.* Wilmette, IL: Daimon.

Shamdasani, S. (Ed.) (1996). *The psychology of Kundalini yoga.* Princeton, NJ: Princeton University Press.

Sidoli, M. (1989). *The unfolding self.* Boston, MA: Sigo Press.

Singer, J. (1994). *Boundaries of the soul.* New York: Anchor Books.

Stein, M. (Ed.), (1995). *Jung on evil.* Princeton, NJ: Princeton University Press.

Stein, M. and Corbett, L. (1991). *Psyche's stories.* Wilmette, IL: Chiron Publications.

Stevens, A. (1990). *On Jung.* London: Penquin Books.

Sullivan, B. (1989). *Psychotherapy grounded in the feminine principle.* Wilmette, IL: Chiron Publications.

Ulanov, A. (1994). *The functioning transcendent: A study in Analytical Psychology.* Wilmette, IL: Chiron Publications.

VonFranz, M.L. (1991). *Individuation in fairy tales*, (Rev. Ed.). Boston, MA: Shambhala Publications.

## CHAPTER POST-INVENTORY

**INSTRUCTIONS: PLEASE ANSWER THE FOLLOWING QUESTIONS NOW THAT YOU HAVE COMPLETED READING THIS CHAPTER:**

T    F    1.   **CARL GUSTAV JUNG** was a cohort of Sigmund Freud.

T    F    2.   An accredited **JUNGIAN TRAINED COUNSELOR** or psychotherapist must undergo intense personal analysis.

T    F    3.   **JUNG'S THEORIES** grew out of his personal background and familial relationships.

T    F    4.   The **COMPLEX** and **ARCHETYPE** are interchangeable.

T    F    5.   **SYMBOLS** are alive with meaning.

T    F    6.   The **PSYCHE** is only a portion of all psychic processes.

T    F    7.   **DREAMS** show the reality of the **PSYCHE**.

T    F    8.   **EGO** is the center of the field of the unconscious.

T    F    9.   The **RELIGIOUS INSTINCT** emanates from the **SELF**.

T    F    10.  **PSYCHIC ENERGY** or **LIBIDO** is found in the conscious mind.

T    F    11.  There are two **FUNCTIONS** and four **ATTITUDES** making up eight typology combinations.

T    F    12.  **DREAMS** only reflect day residues.

T    F    13.  **DREAMS** compensate conscious life.

T    F    14.  Working with the **TRANSFERENCE** is integral to Jungian oriented counseling and psychotherapy.

T    F    15.  Fairy tales reveal the **ARCHETYPAL** process of individuation.

T    F    16.  Myth **MOTIFS** are an aspect of each person's psyche.

T    F    17.  The **EGO** is the regulator of the personality.

**T   F**     18.  Each person has an **ANIMA** and **ANIMUS**.

**T   F**     19.  The **SHADOW** has personal and collective aspects.

**T   F**     20.  When the **PERSONA** is rigid, the **ANIMA** and **ANIMUS** are poorly formed.

# NOTES

# CHAPTER SIX
## *ADLERIAN THEORY*

**CHAPTER PRE-INVENTORY**

**INSTRUCTIONS: PLEASE ANSWER THE FOLLOWING QUESTIONS BEFORE YOU READ THIS CHAPTER:**

T  F  1. Adler rooted his interventions in the values and philosophy of **SOCIAL DE-MOCRACY.**

T  F  2. The Ansbachers, Sadie Dreikurs, Roy Kern, Harold Mosak, Bob Powers, the Pews, the Dinkmeyers, Gary McKay, Jon Carlson, Len Sperry, Margaret Wheeler, and Tom Sweeney are **CONTEMPORARY ADLERIANS.**

T  F  3. Individual's perceptions of their **FAMILY POSITION** have little to do with understanding their outlook on life.  ✓ p 115

T  F  4. **TELEO** denotes the **GOAL-STRIVING** nature of human beings.

T  F  5. The **INDIVISIBILITY** of a person is not a fundamental belief of Individual Psychology.

T  F  6. **ADLER** believed that everyone is confronted by major life tasks.

T  F  7. Adlerians believe that the **LIFE-STYLE** of the individual is a unique, uncon-scious, cognitive map that facilitates one's movement through life.

T  F  8. Adlerians make a distinction between **COUNSELING AND PSYCHOTHER-APY PROCESSES.**

T  F  9. The **FOUR GOALS OF OUR CHILDREN'S DISRUPTIVE BEHAVIOR ARE**: 1) excessive attention seeking, 2) personal power, 3) revenge and 4) retaliation.

T  F  10. **METHODS OF ENCOURAGEMENT** are promoted by Adlerians.

T  F  11. **CARE** is an acronym that summarizes concepts and steps that are helpful to adults living and working with youth.

**T** F    12. When a teacher tells children who persistently forget their pencils that they may not participate in certain writing activities, he has responded with a **LOGICAL CONSEQUENCE**.

**T** F    13. A **LIFE-STYLE ANALYSIS** is an effort to make explicit the attitudes, beliefs, and convictions that one uses in approaching or avoiding life's tasks.

**T** F    14. Typically, **EARLY RECOLLECTIONS** are recorded as part of the interview process following the family constellation.

**T** F    15. **MIDDLE CHILDREN** will most likely establish their uniqueness in directions opposite to their older sibling.

**T** **F**    16. **SECOND CHILDREN** seldom strive to be first in something.

**T** F    17. A **YOUNGEST CHILD** is often described as cute, a charmer, and the family's baby no matter how old he becomes.

**T** F    18. The impact of **BIRTH ORDER** has been studied extensively over the years.

**T** F    19. Few studies related to effective **ELEMENTARY AND SECONDARY APPLICATIONS OF ADLERIAN METHODS** have been reported.

T **F**    20. **CHILDREN: THE CHALLENGE** and **MAINTAINING SANITY IN THE CLASSROOM** were written by Alfred Adler.

# CHAPTER 6 OUTLINE

**CHAPTER SIX**
**Adlerian Theory**

I.  **BACKGROUND**

II. **HUMAN NATURE:  A DEVELOPMENTAL PERSPECTIVE**
    A. Early Development
    B. Family Constellation

III. **MAJOR CONSTRUCTS**
    A. Socio-Teleo-Analytic
       1. Socio
       2. Teleo
       3. Analytic
    B. Holism
    C. Function of Emotions and Feelings

IV. **APPLICATIONS**
    A. Overview
    B. Goals of Counseling and Psychotherapy
       1. Work
       2. Friendship and Love
    C. The process of Change
    D. Intervention Strategies
       1. Encouragement
       2. Parent and Teacher Education
          a. Catch Yourself
          b. Assess Goals
          c. Respond With Consequences and Encouragement
          d. Execute With Consistency, Friendliness, and Respect
       3. Life-style Assessment
       4. Early Recollections

V.  **EVALUATION**
    A. Overview
    B. Supporting Research
       1. Cultural Relevance
       2. Life-Style Studies
       3. Cross-Disciplinary Research
    C. Limitations

## VI. THE CASE OF MARIA: AN ADLERIAN APPROACH

   A. Process Considerations
   B. Establishing Rapport
   C. Psychological Investigation
      1. Individual Characteristics: Family Constellation and Personal Attributes
      2. Adult and Gender Models
      3. Family and Cultural Values
      4. Early Recollections
   D. Interpretation
      1. Approach to Life Tasks
         a. Work
         b. Friendship and Love
         c. Self
         d. Spirituality
      2. Comfort Zone: When Expectations Are Met Versus Unmet
   E. Reorientation
      1. Self-Direction
      2. Work
      3. Friendship
      4. Love
      5. Spirituality
   F. Case of Maria: Caveat

## VII. REFERENCES

## CHAPTER OVERVIEW

The Individual Psychology of Alfred Adler is based upon a phenomenological, holistic understanding of human behavior. It espouses a philosophy of human relations based upon social equality. The practice of Individual Psychology has been characterized as "common sense" and yet, it is still not commonly practiced as Adler intended and modeled. While fundamental principles have remained the same, new techniques and applications and the evolution of theory continue into the twenty-first century.

This chapter briefly overviews the history of Individual Psychology and includes mention of the work of not only Alfred Adler and Rudolf Dreikurs but also that of the Ansbachers, Sadie Dreikurs, Harold Mosak, Bob Powers, the Pews, the Dinkmeyers, Gary McKay, Jon Carlson, Len Sperry and Tom Sweeney. Early development and the importance of the family constellation provide the emphasis for a discussion of human development. Constructs such as the socio-teleo-analytic nature of human beings, life tasks, the function of emotion and feelings and holism from an Adlerian perspective is followed by a discussion of the goals of counseling, the process of change and intervention strategies. The author emphasizes the distinction between Adlerian counseling and psychotherapy. In the case of counseling, behavior change within the existing life style is the goal. In psychotherapy, a change of life style is the desired outcome.

A discussion of encouragement methods, parent and teacher education, and life-style assessment are followed by an overview of supporting research, limitations, an overview chart and a presentation of the "Case of Maria."

## KEY TERMS

Private Logic
Family constellation
The five ordinal positions
Socio
Teleo
Analytic
Life tasks
Discouragement
Function of feelings and emotions
Holistic view
Life style
Adlerian counseling

Adlerian psychotherapy
Goals of disruptive behavior
Encouragement
CARE
Catch yourself
Questions to assess goals
Natural consequences
Logical consequences
Life style assessment
Stages in Adlerian counseling
Early recollections
"Spitting in the client's soup"

## KEY PEOPLE

A. Adler
R. Ansbacher
D. Dinkmeyer
R. Dreikurs
G. McKay
W. Pew
L. Sperry

H. Ansbacher
J. Carlson
D. Dinkmeyer, Jr.
S. Dreikurs
H. Mosak
B. Powers
T. Sweeney

## INDIVIDUAL EXERCISES TO ENHANCE STUDENTS' LEARNING

1. A counselor's or therapist's effectiveness is enhanced if he/she understands the goals of children's disruptive behavior. Discuss the Adlerian concept of the goals of disruptive behavior. What are the four questions adults can ask to help assess the goals of children's behavior?

2. Understanding the family constellation and the five key ordinal positions can be used as tools by Adlerians in the process of working with clients. What is your understanding of the Adlerian concept of the family constellation? Do you find the descriptions of the five ordinal positions useful?

3. Describe some of the methods of encouragement presented in chapter six. Have you attempted to use any of these? What results have you achieved through the use of encouragement techniques? How do you respond to others' use of encouragement with you?

4. What is the difference between natural and logical consequences?

5. Discuss the Adlerian concept of "life style."

## CLASSROOM EXERCISES TO ENHANCE INSTRUCTION AND STUDENT LEARNING

### INTERVENTION #1: INDIVIDUAL PSYCHOLOGY

1. Intervention/condition: Care.

2. Purpose of Intervention: To help adults learn new ways of responding to children's misbehavior.

3. Classroom Procedures:

a. Review CARE including the descriptions in the chapter:
   1) Catch yourself: don't act impulsively.
   2) Assess goals--what goals are served by the behavior?
   3) Respond with consequences and encouragement.
   4) Execute with consistency, friendliness, and respect.
b. Divide class into units of three or four.
c. Have each member of the groups describe a situation that they have witnessed in which a youngster has misbehaved. Have them select one upon which to develop a CARE plan.
d. Together they should attempt to:
   1) Describe what adults typically do when it happens and what they can do even if it is just to stop what they have been doing.
   2) Identify the goal of misbehavior, what the child must be saying to him/herself, what the adults feel when it happens. (Note: all misbehavior draws some attention to the child, simply identifying all misbehavior as attention seeking misses the underlying motivation of much misbehavior.)
   3) Choose two or more natural and/or logical consequences for implementation.
   4) Specifically describe who, when, and how these can be used. (Note: attempt to ascertain that the consequences meet the conditions for logically following the nature of the misbehavior, are nonpunitive, not done in anger, allow responsible choices, etc.)
   5) Likewise, specify both verbal and nonverbal encouragement activities to be used by whom, when, and how. (Note: praise of the person is not considered "encouragement." Also, if at all possible, it is better to intervene positively before misbehavior must be handled).
e. Each group is invited to present their plan and receive feedback from the group on additions, modifications, etc.
f. If the plan can be implemented in the coming week, the class can hear about the effects the next week. (Naturally, the implementation will be only a small effort in attempting to redirect an individual or group and will require critique, refinement, etc.)

4. Indications for use: Typical misbehavior found in home and schools.

5. Contraindications: Adults who are functioning from a highly authoritarian structure for whom the interventions could be construed as another type of manipulation and exertion of power.

6. Source:
Sweeney, T.J. (1989) *Adlerian Counseling*. Muncie, IN: Accelerated Development, Inc.

7. Additional Readings:
Dreikurs, R. and Grey, L. (1968). *Logical Consequences*. New York: Hawthorn Books.

# INTERVENTION #2: INDIVIDUAL PSYCHOLOGY

1. Intervention/Condition: Family Constellation.

2. Purpose of Intervention: To help trainees validate the usefulness of family constellation data in counseling and consultation with individuals and families.

3. Classroom Procedures:
   a. Review the family constellation section of the chapter including descriptions of the five ordinal positions:
      1) Identify each family position for members of the class, i.e., only, oldest, second, middle, and youngest. (Note: siblings more than six years apart are not typically in the same constellation; e.g., two siblings seven years apart have grown up more like two only children.)
      2) In large classes, have each sibling position group together; i.e., oldest, only, etc. In smaller classes, oldest and only may be grouped together; youngest and second, likewise. Middle "kids" will tell you, they do not "group"!
      3) Ask the groups to recall their early (before eight years old) recollection of what it was like to be in their position in the family. What was it like? How did they feel about that position when they were that age? What did they think and feel about the advantages and disadvantages for them and for their sibling's positions?
      4) Invite each group to share their perceptions (this is worth a lot of laughs if they really get into it!).
      5) Invite a class member with more than one or more siblings to volunteer to describe his/her family constellation. Simply use the blackboard to record the names of the class member and his/her siblings across the top of the board. Then, remind the members to recount only how they remember each member as they were as youngsters, use the following outline:
         a) Ordinal Position-List all the children in the family in their birth order and list their ages plus or minus years compared to the member's age, including siblings now dead and/or miscarriages which were known to the person as a child. For example:

         > Bill + 2
         > Ted 26 (interviewee)
         > Marge - 2
         > girl baby - 3 (stillborn)
         > Sue - 10

         (In this example, Ted is a middle child in a two family constellation; i.e., Sue is more likely to have the characteristics of the only child because she is more than six to eight years younger than the next sibling.
         b) Descriptions of Siblings--Be specific in description: Who is most different from you? In what respect (likely competitor)? Who is most like you? In what respect (possible ally)? What kind of kid were you? Describe the other siblings.

70

c) Comparative Attributes--Rate self and siblings on each of the following attributes by indicating who you believed was highest or most, who was lowest or least. If you were neither one, indicate to which sibling you were most similar: Intelligence, Tried to please, Hardest worker, Got own way, Best grades in school, Sense of humor, Helped at home, High standards, Conforming, Most spoiled, Rebellious, Most punished.

d) Sibling Relationship: Who took care of whom? Who played with whom? Who was favorite of mother? Father? Who got along best and who fought most?

e) Parent: Parent ages? What kind of person was each? Which child liked father most? Mother most? In what ways? What kind of relationship existed between father and mother? Who was more ambitious for the children? In what ways? Did any other persons live with or significantly influence you?

6) It may not be necessary to proceed beyond the characteristics of the siblings to establish that there tends to be a pattern among the positions in the family. Having the characteristics in mind, a discussion can be conducted concerning the application of these insights for parent education, family consultation on child rearing, and establishing rapport with youngsters whom you have just met. Naturally, it is applicable with adults as well. It is important to remind the class that the principle in operation has to do with each sibling making a unique place for her/himself. When individuals do not share the common characteristics of their birth position, Adlerians still find that the principle is in operation, you just have to know to continue looking for how it applies to these individuals.

4. Indications for use: To quickly establish rapport and to confirm or refute hunches about such characteristics for a specific individual.

5. Contraindications: The demonstration must be with sensitivity to matters of confidentiality of the volunteer/client and no expectation for them to answer any questions which they consider inappropriate under the circumstances.

6. Source: Sweeney, T.J. (1989) *Adlerian Counseling*. Muncie, IN: Accelerated Development, Inc.

7. Additional Readings: Shulman, B.H. & Mosak, H.H. (1988). *Life Style Inventory*. Muncie, IN: Accelerated Development, Inc.
Shulman, B.H. & Mosak, H.H. (1988). *Manual for LifeStyle Assessment*. Muncie, IN: Accelerated Development, Inc.

*INTERVENTION #3: INDIVIDUAL PSYCHOLOGY*

1. Intervention/Condition: Early Recollections.

2. Purpose of Intervention: To help trainees validate the usefulness of early recollection data in counseling with individuals and couples.

3. Classroom Procedures:
   a. Review the life style section of the chapter including, especially, that related to early recollections.
   b. Provide class members time to write out three to six early recollections exactly as they remember them with particular attention to their feeling at the time (this could be a homework assignment). They should recount them in as much detail as they can recall but even short, seemingly inconsequential, incidents can be useful. Remind them of the differences between a specific early recollection and a report of general happenings.
   c. Invite a volunteer to sit in front of the class and share early recollections in their own words. Have another class member write them on the board verbatim. Then invite the class to guess what the self talk of the individual might be, i.e., based upon such as the following:
   1) In these recollections:
      a) Is the individual active or passive?
      b) Is he/she an observer or participant?
      c) Is he/she giving or taking?
      d) Does he/she go forth or withdraw?
      e) What is his/her physical posture or position in relation to what is around him?
      f) Is he/she alone or with others?
      g) Is his/her concern with people, things, or ideas? Located outside or in a room, house, etc.?
      h) What relationship does he/she place himself/herself into with others? Inferior? Superior?
      I) What emotion does he/she use?
      j) What feeling tone is attached to the event or outcome? Is detail and color mentioned?
      k) Do stereotypes of authorities, subordinates, men, women, old, young, reveal themselves?
      l) Prepare a "headline" which captures the essence of the event; for example: Girl Gets Job Done!
      m) Look for themes and an overall pattern.
      n) Look for corroboration in the family constellation information if available. The volunteer should be the only source of the correctness of the observations. When an observation is "right," you will normally see a knowing smile or laugh. Encourage guessing but caution against "analysis" and interpretation, per se. Also encourage the volunteer to help modify the words and phrases to make them "fit" if someone is close

but not quite on. Also suggest that when a statement fits that an illustration of how it is reflected in behavior could be helpful.

4. <u>Indications for use</u>: To gain insight into the motivation and self talk unique to an individual.

5. <u>Contraindications</u>: The demonstration must be with sensitivity to matters of confidentiality of the volunteer/client and no expectation for them to answer any questions which they consider inappropriate under the circumstances.

6. <u>Source</u>: Sweeney, T.J. (1989). *Adlerian Counseling*. Muncie, IN: Accelerated Development, Inc.

7. <u>Additional Readings</u>: Shulman, B.H. & Mosak, H.H. (1988). *Life Style Inventory*. Muncie, IN: Accelerated Development, Inc.
Shulman, B.H. & Mosak, H.H. (1988). *Manual for Life Style Assessment*. Muncie, IN: Accelerated Development, Inc.
Sweeney, T.J. (1990). Early recollections: A promising technique for use with older people, *Journal of Mental Health Counseling*. 12(3) 260-69.
Sweeney, T.J. & Myers, J.E. (1989). *Group work with older persons: A videotape and study guide*. Greensboro, NC: New Hope Enterprise.

## QUESTIONS FOR STUDY AND DISCUSSION

1. As you review chapter six, how would you summarize the major contributions of the Adlerian approach to counseling and psychotherapy?

2. What have you learned about yourself in relation to your position in your family constellation? How will these insights help you be a more effective counselor?

3. Can you think of an instance in which awareness of the four goals of misbehavior would have helped you be more effective with a child or an adolescent?

4. Summarize the subsection of chapter six that reports the supporting research and explain how this information could impact your application of Adlerian principles.

5. What do you see as the relationship between your own personality characteristics and your selection or rejection of Individual Psychology as the conceptual frame of reference to guide your "practice" with clients?

**SUGGESTED READINGS**

Ansbacher, H. L., & Ansbacher, R. R. (Eds.). (1967). *The individual psychology of Alfred Adler*. New York: Harper & Row.

Crandall, J. E. (1991). Life style can be measured. *Individual Psychology: Journal of Adlerian Theory, Research, and Practice*, *47*, 229-240.

Dreikurs, R. (1946). *The challenge of marriage*. New York: Hawthorne.

Dreikurs, R. (1968). *Psychology in the classroom* (2nd ed.). New York: Harper & Row.

Sweeney, T. J. (1998). *Adlerian counseling: A practitioner's approach*. (4th ed.). Muncie, IN: Accelerated Development.

Witmer, J. M., & Sweeney, T. J. (1992). A holistic model for wellness and prevention over the life span. *Journal of Counseling and Development*, *71*(2), 140148.

## CHAPTER POST-INVENTORY

**INSTRUCTIONS: PLEASE ANSWER THE FOLLOWING QUESTIONS NOW THAT YOU HAVE COMPLETED READING THIS CHAPTER.**

**(T)** F    1. Adler rooted his interventions in the values and philosophy of **SOCIAL DE-MOCRACY.**

**(T)** F    2. The Ansbachers, Sadie Dreikurs, Roy Kern, Harold Mosak, Bob Powers, the Pews, the Dinkmeyers, Gary McKay, Jon Carlson, Len Sperry, Margaret Wheeler, and Tom Sweeney are **CONTEMPERARY ADLERIANS.**

T **(F)**    3. Individual's perceptions of their **FAMILY POSITION** have little to do with understanding their outlook on life.

**(T)** F    4. **TELEO** denotes the **GOAL-STRIVING** nature of human beings.

T **(F)**    5. The **INDIVISIBILITY** of a person is not a fundamental belief of Individual Psychology.

**(T)** F    6. **ADLER** believed that everyone is confronted by major life tasks.

**(T)** F    7. Adlerians believe that the **LIFE-STYLE** of the individual is a unique, unconscious, cognitive map that facilitates one's movement through life.

**(T)** F    8. Adlerians make a distinction between **COUNSELING AND PSYCHOTHERAPY PROCESSES..**

T **(F)**    9. The **FOUR GOALS OF OUR CHILDREN'S DISRUPTIVE BEHAVIOR ARE**: 1) excessive attention seeking, 2) personal power, 3) revenge and 4) retalliation.

**(T)** F    10. **METHODS OF ENCOURAGEMENT** are promoted by Adlerians.

**(T)** F    11. **CARE** is an acronnym that summarizes concepts and steps that are helpful to adults living and working with youth.

T **(F)**    12. When a teacher tells children who persistently forget their pencils that they may not participate in certain writing activities, he has responded with a **LOGICAL CONSEQUENCE.**

**(T)** F    13. A **LIFE-STYLE ANALYSIS** is an effort to make explicit the attitudes, beliefs, and convictions that one use in approaching or avoiding life's tasks.

(T) F    14. Typically, **EARLY RECOLLECTIONS** are recorded as part of the interview process following the family constellation.

(T) F    15. **MIDDLE CHILDREN** will most likely establish their uniqueness in directions opposite to their older sibling.

T (F)    16. **SECOND CHILDREN** seldom strive to be first in something.

(T) F    17. A **YOUNGEST CHILD** is often described as cute, a charmer, and the family's baby no matter how old he becomes.

(T) F    18. The impact of **BIRTH ORDER** has been studied extensively over the years.

T (F)    19. Few studies related to effective **ELEMENTARY AND SECONDARY APPLICATIONS OF ADLERIAN METHODS** have been reported.

T (F)    20. **CHILDREN: THE CHALLENGE** and **MAINTAINING SANITY IN THE CLASSROOM** were written by Alfred Adler.

# CHAPTER SEVEN
## EXISTENTIAL THEORY

**CHAPTER PRE-INVENTORY**

**INSTRUCTIONS: PLEASE ANSWER THE FOLLOWING QUESTIONS BEFORE YOU READ THIS CHAPTER:**

T　F　　　1. Frankl would be considered an **EXISTENTIALIST.**

T　F　　　2. In existential theory, confronting **EXISTENTIAL QUESTIONS** can be painful.

T　F　　　3. The **I-YOU RELATIONSHIP** serves as the basis for existential counseling.

T　F　　　4. Unlike the **PSYCHOANALYTIC AND PSYCHODYNAMIC THEORIES,** existentialists are deficiency focused.

T　F　　　5. According to **KIERKEGAARD,** human problems exist not due to lack of knowledge or technology, but due to lack of passion and commitment.

T　F　　　6. Although **EXISTENTIAL ISSUES** can arise in adulthood, most existential concerns are salient in childhood.

T　F　　　7. In existentialism, ego development and defense structures provide the framework for understanding **DEATH ANXIETY**.

T　F　　　8. The relationship level called " **WE-WE** " is generally found in adulthood.

T　F　　　9. **EXISTENTIAL COUNSELING** could probably be worked into a computer program.

T　F　　　10. **EXISTENTIALISTS** have not found a way to work with other theories of counseling.

T　F　　　11. A **"HAZARD"** of being an existential counselor includes a need to protect private time and space.

T　F　　　12. Saying **"GOOD BYE"** is not a very important part of the counseling process.

T　F　　　13. Telling the **STORY OF OUR LIFE** can be a helpful way to gain perspective.

T   F     14. Often existential clients feel **GUILTY** over what they have not accomplished as well as for what they have done.

T   F     15. **CULTURE** and **GENDER** have little place in an existential perspective.

T   F     16. The understanding of **OUR RESPONSIBILITY** is important to the existential journey.

T   F     17. **EXISTENTIAL COUNSELORS** have established a strong body of research.

T   F     18. Living **AUTHENTICALLY** simply means being honest with your client.

T   F     19. Existential counseling is **"TRAGICALLY OPTIMISTIC."**

T   F     20. In existentialism **"DEATH"** is the ultimate truth.

**CHAPTER SEVEN**
**Existential Theory**

I.      **BACKGROUND**

II.     **HUMAN NATURE:  A DEVELOPMENTAL  PERSPECTIVE**
      A.  Psychopathology
      B.  A World View

III.    **MAJOR CONSTRUCTS**
      A.  Approaches to Existentialism
      B.  Death
      C.  Freedom
      D.  Isolation
      E.  Culture
      F.  Meaninglessness/Meaningfulness
      G.  Authenticity and Vulnerability: Two Sides of the Existential Self
      H.  Existential Relationships
      H.  Hazards on the Journey

IV.     **APPLICATIONS**
      A.  Overview
      B.  Goals of counseling and psychotherapy
      C.  The Process of Change
      D.  Intervention Strategies
         1.  Telling the Story: Finding the Meaning of Myth
         2.  Sharing Existence in the Moment
         3.  Centered Awareness of Being
         4.  Self-Responsibility
         5.  Dream Work
         6.  Disclosing and Working Through Resistances
         7.  Confronting Existential Anxiety
         8.  Sustaining Changes in Being
         9.  Separating

V.      **EVALUATION**
      A.  Overview
      B.  Supporting Research
         1.  Using Testing to Measure Existential Conflict
      C.  Limitations

**VI. THE CASE OF MARIA: AN EXISTENTIAL APPROACH**
   A. Treatment/Intervention Plan
   B. Case Analysis

**VII. REFERENCES**

## CHAPTER OVERVIEW

The primary confrontation with death was addressed by the existential philosophers and has found life in the existential therapies. Rollo May (1969a), in examining the roots of existential thought, indicated that the term existentialism derived from "exsistere," meaning to "stand out" or "to emerge". The theory of existentialism is an emergent part of the third force of psychology, attempting to look at the deeper meanings of our lives.

The existential perspective is not simplistic nor technique driven. The existential theorist and therapist explore themselves when they look at the concerns of others. The emphasis is on existence not essence. From this perspective, it is more important to understand and experience the person in the moment, rather than examining the essential parts. We all experience ontological insecurities, existential anxieties, and fear of ultimate meaninglessness. Existential theory provides a theoretical basis from which to address these basic concerns.

Whether we are more present in the world or transcend our given situations, we are more aware, alive, and connected. We emerge from a confrontation with ultimate reality with a renewed sense of purpose, understanding, and hope. Embodying the original intent of "psyche" ology (MacLeod, 1975), existentialism is most truly a study of the individual's soul.

## KEY TERMS

Angst
Anxiety
Authenticity
Being in the world
Culture
Dasien
Death
Death anxiety
Depression
Dreamwork
Dynamic existentialism
Empathy
Essence
Ex-sistere
Existence
Existential questions
Existential anxiety
Existential relationship
Existential journey
Existential isolation
Experiential awareness

Freedom
Gender
Guilt
Humanism
Humanistic existentialism
I-Thou relationship
I-you relationship
Isolation
Loss of self
Loss of the world
Meaning
Meaninglessness
Non-existence
Ontological anxiety
Responsibility
Search for meaning
Spirituality
Third force psychology
Transcendence
Transpersonal existentialism

## KEY PEOPLE

L. Binswanger

J. Bugental

M. Buber

V. Frankl

N. Heidigger

S. Kierkegaard

E. Kubler-Ross

J. Lantz

D. Loy

A. Maslow

R. May

F. Neitzsche

J. Sartre

P. Tillich

K. Wilber

R. Willis

I. Yalom

## CLASSROOM EXERCISES TO ENHANCE INSTRUCTION AND STUDENT LEARNING

1. Why counseling? The existential focus is on the training of the counselor rather than a "technique" to be used with a client. If used with a client, it would need to flow from the understanding of the client's needs, rather than be an intervention to illicit a response. The purpose of this exercise is to help beginning counselors/ therapists understand the importance of the I-Thou relationship in their own development, to examine what motivations lie behind their choice to be a counselor/ therapist, and to begin understanding the relationship dynamics that facilitate an existential therapeutic relationship. The class begins with the instructor leading a discussion of the reasons people enter the helping fields of counseling, therapy, teaching, etc. Discuss relationships that students in class have had that facilitated that choice. Encourage students to write down the nature of the encounter and the quality of the relationship. In the process of having the students discuss the nature of the relationship, discuss the elements that were the most effectual, what made the relationship meaningful? What can the students learn from that relationship and offer others?

2. The instructor distributes a rock (or a shell or a basket of items) to each student in class. Tell each student that the rock is their client and ask them to take the next few minutes to spend time with their client. After about ten minutes, bring the class back together. What did people "do" with (to) their client? How was the experience for them? What was their first inclination when told the assignment? (e.g. some people generally want to "fix" what is wrong, some fidget with the rock and don't know what to do, others poke and explore the rock). How might this parallel the first experience with a "real" client. How did the "client" feel about the inquiry?

3. Ask the students to get into small groups for discussion of this exercise. Encourage them to write two obituaries: one that would be written about them now and one that they hope can be written about them in the future. What is different about the

two? Would you live differently now if you knew that you didn't have long to live? How different would that make your life?

4. Getting students in small groups, ask them to talk about their views of death. Ask them to look at the way our culture/society approaches death and how it feels to discuss it in a classroom. Also ask students to look at the work by Kubler-Ross and others about the stages of death and dying. Discuss current research in this area.

5. Review the ways in which studying existential concerns might change a person. How is it to read about the concepts in Chapter 7? How did you feel about the importance of relationships and the struggle to gain meaning in life? How do you resolve your reactions to death, freedom, isolation, and meaninglessness? How does the theory apply?

6. Classroom Procedures: Distribute blank paper (different colors are best) to the class. Each student takes one sheet. Markers/crayons/or any other media are helpful. Ask students to draw a mask they wear as a student or as a counselor/ therapist. Discuss as a class the masks worn by the students. What masks do you wear? What is underneath the masks? What are your idealized or despised images that are on the mask(s)? What keeps the mask in place and what would happen if you were to remove the mask?

## INDIVIDUAL EXERCISES TO ENHANCE THE STUDENTS' LEARNING

1. Ask students to keep a journal of their thoughts/reactions to this course. Have them write an entry for each chapter and outline their personal reactions to "trying on" these concepts. At the end of the term, require students to write a "developmental" paper about their growth over the course of the term. What thoughts did they notice they had early in the term? How did they change or evolve? What impact did the theories have on them and their life? Which approach did they like best? What do they think is their personal reason for that choice?

2. If possible, interview various therapists to discover their "theoretical orientations." What approaches are used most often? In what settings do they work? How do they address issues of loss? How do they believe people change?

3. Visit a nursing home (volunteer a few hours a week if possible). Spend time with one or two of the people at the home and find out about their life. What was most important to them? What is most important now? What do they feel they accomplished?

4. Visit a Hospice organization. How do they get referrals? Interview a case worker. What is it like for them working with people who are dying? What are the most difficult people with whom they work? What do they like about their work?

5. Taking any magazine, look through it (don't miss the advertisements!) to find the things that are seen as most important in life. What is the way we are supposed to achieve happiness? What is success? How do these things compare with the interviews you had in questions 2, 3, or 4? How do we resolve these discrepancies for ourselves?

## QUESTIONS FOR STUDY AND DISCUSSION

1. What is meant by the statement, "Existentialists were the 'homeless waifs' who were not permitted into the better academic neighborhoods" (Yalom, 1980, p.21)?

2. What is meant by the concept "world view" as presented in existential literature?

3. What are your views on the emphasis that existentialism places on the role of death in counseling and therapy?

4. What are the similarities and differences between Humanistic Existentialism, Dynamic Existentialism and Transpersonal Existentialism?

5. What is the role of spiritual or religious thought in counseling? How does it fit in the historical development of theories? What is the impact of allowing spiritual questions to enter into the counseling process?

## SUGGESTED READINGS

Abroms, E. M. (1993). *The freedom of the self: The bio-existential treatment of character problems*. New York: Plenum Publishing Corporation.

Bender, S. (1996). *Everyday sacred: A woman's journey home*. San Francisco: Harper.

Bolen, J.S. (1996). *Close to the bone: Life-threatening illness and the search for meaning*. New York: Scribner.

Dass, R., & Gordon, P. (1985). *How Can I Help*. New York: Alfred A. Knopf.

DeMello, A. (1988). *A Book of Story Meditations*. New York: Doubleday.

Frankl, V. (1984). *Man's search for meaning*. New York: Washington Square Press.

Kopp, S. (1972). *If You Meet the Buddha on the Road, Kill Him*. New York: Bantam Books.

Lantz, J. (1993). *Existential family therapy*. Northvale, NJ: Jason Aronson.

May, R. (1992). *The cry for myth*. New York: Delta.

Meier, S., & Davis, S. (1997). *The Elements of Counseling* (3rd ed.). Pacific Grove, CA: Brooks/Cole Publishing.

Yalom, I. (1972). *Every Day Gets a Little Closer*. New York: Basic Books.

Yalom, I. (1989). *Love's Executioner and Other Tales of Psychotherapy*. New York: Basic

Yalom, I. (1992). *When Nietzsche wept*. New York: Basic Books.

## CHAPTER POST-INVENTORY

**INSTRUCTIONS: PLEASE ANSWER THE FOLLOWING QUESTIONS NOW THAT YOU HAVE COMPLETED READING THIS CHAPTER.**

T  F  1. Frankl would be considered an **EXISTENTIALIST.**

T  F  2. In existential theory, confronting **EXISTENTIAL QUESTIONS** can be painful.

T  F  3. The **I-YOU RELATIONSHIP** serves as the basis for existential counseling.

T  F  4. Unlike the **PSYCHOANALYTIC AND PSYCHODYNAMIC THEORIES,** existentialists are deficiency focused.

T  F  5. According to **KIERKEGAARD,** human problems exist not due to lack of knowledge or technology, but due to lack of passion and commitment.

T  F  6. Although **EXISTENTIAL ISSUES** can arise in adulthood, most existential concerns are salient in childhood.

T  F  7. In existentialism, ego development and defense structures provide the framework for understanding **DEATH ANXIETY**.

T  F  8. The relationship level called " **WE-WE** " is generally found in adulthood.

T  F  9. **EXISTENTIAL COUNSELING** could probably be worked into a computer program.

T  F  10. **EXISTENTIALISTS** have not found a way to work with other theories of counseling.

T  F  11. A **"HAZARD"** of being an existential counselor includes a need to protect private time and space.

T  F  12. Saying **"GOOD BYE"** is not a very important part of the counseling process.

T  F  13. Telling the **STORY OF OUR LIFE** can be a helpful way to gain perspective.

T  F  14. Often existential clients feel **GUILTY** over what they have not accomplished as well as for what they have done.

T  F  15. **CULTURE** and **GENDER** have little place in an existential perspective.

T  F  16. The understanding of **OUR RESPONSIBILITY** is important to the existential journey.

T  F  17. **EXISTENTIAL COUNSELORS** have established a strong body of research.

T  F  18. Living **AUTHENTICALLY** simply means being honest with your client.

T  F  19. Existential counseling is **"TRAGICALLY OPTIMISTIC."**

T  F  20. In existentialism "**DEATH**" is the ultimate truth.

# CHAPTER EIGHT
## _PERSON-CENTERED THEORY_

**CHAPTER PRE-INVENTORY**

**INSTRUCTIONS: PLEASE ANSWER THE FOLLOWING QUESTIONS BEFORE YOU READ THIS CHAPTER.**

(T)   F   ✓   1. The **PERSON-CENTERED THEORIST** views people as fully in charge of their lives and inherently motivated to improve themselves.

(T)   F   ✓   2. The **PHENOMENOLOGICAL PERSPECTIVE** refers to the uniqueness of each person's perspective.

T   (F)   3. The goal of **SELF-ACTUALIZATION** is achievement of perfection as a human.   _primary motivational strength behind development_

(T)   F   ✓   4. Rogers believed that harmful thoughts and actions were reflections of a distorted view of self and the world.

✗ (T)   F   5. One major limitation of person-centered theory is the lack of **EMPIRICAL RESEARCH** establishing its effectiveness.

(T)   F   6. A **POSITIVE VIEW OF HUMAN NATURE** is essential for the person-centered practitioner because of the major responsibilities clients are given in the direction, style, and content of counseling.

✗ (T)   F   7. The counselor's role in person-centered counseling is to help the client **BE-COME** good, constructive, and trustworthy.

(T)   F   8. Rogers believed that people use defensive thoughts and actions to protect themselves from **INCONGRUENCE**.

(T)   F   9. The **ESSENTIAL GOAL** for people experiencing psychological or sociological difficulties is to perceive their own positive nature more accurately and learn to use it more effectively in their everyday lives.

(T)   (F)   10. When individuals make judgments based upon expectations of others rather than their own best judgment, they are responding to perceived **CONDITIONS OF WORTH**.

T   (F)   11. **UNCONDITIONAL POSITIVE REGARD** should only be expressed when individuals have earned such regard with appropriate behaviors.

T (F) 12. **PERSON-CENTERED THEORY** involves numerous techniques.

T (F) 13. Empathic understanding refers only to the counselor's understanding of the client's world from the client's **PHENOMENOLGICAL PERSPECTIVE.**

(T) F 14. The person-centered practitioner treats the client as an **EFFECTIVE HUMAN BEING** who will succeed regardless of the nature of his/her difficulties.

(T) F 15. A major objective in person-centered therapy is to achieve **CONGRUENCE.**

(T) F 16. Rogers believed that the **CORE CONDITIONS** (genuineness, unconditional positive regard, and empathic understanding) provide the necessary environment that allows individuals to implement their actualizing tendencies.

T (F) 17. **INTERNAL LOCI OF CONTROL** develop when clients experience anxiety caused by internalizing "shoulds and oughts" from others running their lives.

X T (F) 18. **PERSON-CENTERED THEORY** is much more related to who a counselor is than to what a counselor does.

T (F) 19. Being a **GENUINE** counselor means sharing every thought and feeling with a client.

T (F) 20. **ACTIVE LISTENING** is the simple act of taking in information from the client.

# CHAPTER 8 OUTLINE

**CHAPTER EIGHT**
**Person-Centered Theory**

I. **BACKGROUND**
   A. Carl R. Rogers
   B. Theory Background

II. **HUMAN NATURE:  A DEVELOPMENTAL PERSPECTIVE**
   A. People Are Trustworthy
   B. Movement Toward Actualization
   C. Inner Resources
   D. Individually Perceived World
   E. Interaction With External Factors

III. **MAJOR CONSTRUCTS**
   A. No Two People See the World Exactly Alike
   B. Empathic Understanding
   C. People Make Simple Mistakes in Judgment
   D. Confidence in the Client
   E. Perceived World of the Client May Not Approximate the World Sought
   F. Congruent Individuals Trust Their World View

IV. **APPLICATIONS**
   A. Overview
   B. Goals of Counseling and Psychotherapy
   C. The Process of Change
   D. Intervention Strategies
      1. Being Genuine
      2. Active Listening
      3. Reflection of Content and Feelings
      4. Appropriate Self-Disclosure
      5. Immediacy
      6. Personalized Counselor Actions
      7. Non-Client-Centered Interventions

V. **EVALUATION**
   A. Overview
   B. Supporting Research
   C. Limitations

## VI. THE CASE OF MARIA: A PERSON-CENTERED APPROACH
A. Maria's Phenomenological World
B. Actualizing Tendencies
C. The Counselor's Role
D. Expectations for Progress

## VII. REFERENCES

## CHAPTER OVERVIEW

Person-centered theory has become one of the most popular theories of counseling and therapy since it developed in the 1940s. It was first labeled nondirective by its originator, Carl Rogers. The theory offered a distinct alternative to the behavioral and psychoanalytic theories that dominated psychology at the time. Rogers later broadened the concepts of the process and renamed it client-centered to de-emphasize the nondirective nature and emphasize a full understanding of all the client's dimensions. The person-centered concept evolved as issues relating to equality of participants in the relationship and a focus on the positive health of people as opposed to a more unhealthy client status became significant issues.

Person-centered theory makes possible the expansion of helping situations. Originally developed as an individual process, it has since become a major group theory. This group focus has expanded into concepts popular in education. Rogers' most recent work emphasized the same concepts as ways of dealing with international conflict resolution in an emphasis on promoting world peace.

Person-centered theory places great emphasis on the individual's ability to move in positive directions. Practitioners of the theory have a belief in the trustworthiness of individuals and in their innate ability to move toward self-actualization and health when the proper conditions are in place. Tied to these beliefs is the confidence that individuals also have the inner resources to move themselves in such positive directions. Finally, a core concept in the theory states that individuals perceive the world in a unique phenomenological way so that no two people's perceptions of the world are the same.

The perception of clients as competent, trustworthy, and forward-moving people who have their own unique view of the world places great confidence in the individual's ability to control his/her own positive change. This confidence in the client directs the counselor to provide the conditions for that change. Specifically, there are three basic conditions needed to support an individual's natural inclination for positive growth: a genuine relationship with a relatively congruent individual, acceptance and caring from the counselor, and an accurate understanding on the part of the counselor of the client's phenomenological world.

Clients who are provided with these growth conditions will realize their actualizing tendencies for growth. They will explore their difficulties and natural competencies in this productive environment, which will then lead to a clearer picture of themselves and their potential. As clients' pictures of themselves become more accurate, they become better able to act in ways that are most in line with their true self (congruence). This in turn will lead to more self-confidence, self-understanding, and better choices.

The role of the counselor in person-centered theory is primarily to promote the conditions for change rather than do things to bring about specific changes. Counselors and therapists are expected to maintain a genuine human relationship in which they provide unconditional positive regard to their clients. This demonstrates their faith in clients and support of the process. Much of the work of the person-centered counselor revolves around developing an accurate empathic understanding of a client, conveying that understanding to the person, and working with him to expand and clarify the understanding and its impact on the client's choices and actions.

Rogers' work initiated much research on the helping relationship and client gain. The use of taping and transcriptions to evaluate the necessary conditions of counseling and psychotherapy received emphasis from research on this theory. A great deal of innovative research in the area of clinical growth was also produced in the development of this theory. However, much of this theory has been integrated into the overall body of the theory, and relatively little research is currently being done in the area. Calls are being made for potential expansion of the theory and research into its future development. Person-centered counseling and psychotherapy has given much to the field, and professionals continue to emphasize the need for growth of the theory rather than a stagnant use of the theory's many positive contributions.

## KEY TERMS

Person-centered                         Phenomenological perspective
Actualize                               Nondirective
Client-centered Therapy                 Trustworthy
Self-actualization                      View of self
Real self                               Autonomy
Unconditional positive regard           Conditions of worth
Empathy                                 Empathic understanding
Incongruence                            Congruence
Core conditions                         Genuineness
Internal loci of control                Immediacy

## KEY PEOPLE

A. Boy                                  C. Rogers
D. Cain                                 L. Thayer
N. Watson                               G. Pine

## CLASSROOM EXERCISES TO ENHANCE INSTRUCTION AND STUDENT LEARNING

1. Divide the class into groups of three asking one group member to act as a person-centered counselor, one member act as client, and the other member observer. The "client" is instructed to bring forth a fictional problem while the "counselor" attempts to demonstrate active listening. After ten minutes, each group discusses the experience (e.g. How did it feel to be the client? The counselor? What worked, what didn't, etc.) After discussion in groups, the "counselor" of each group moves to a different group and becomes the "counselor." This time, however, the therapist uses a

directive, problem-solving approach to the client's problem (e.g. Have you tried such and such? Why don't you do such and such, etc.) After ten minutes. each group discusses the experience (e.g. How did it feel to be the client? The counselor, etc.) Following group discussions, each group shares their feelings about the differences in experiences with the class.

2. Using the same format as above, practice immediacy (e.g. How are you feeling now? This is how your statements make me feel, etc.)

3. Divide the class into teams and ask each team to prepare a list of the types of problems that (or "diagnostic" categories) would benefit most from person-centered therapy. Which populations might not be best served by this approach alone? Conduct a total group discussion at the end of the presentation.

## INDIVIDUAL EXERCISES TO ENHANCE STUDENTS' LEARNING

1. Based upon your specific population of interest, conduct library research to determine if the person-centered approach would be sufficiently effective for treatment. Why or why not?

2. Make a list of your personal values. Consider the extent to which your lifestyle is or is not a reflection of those values?

3. Make a list of values clients may expose which are opposing to yours. Would it be difficult for you to experience and express unconditional positive regard toward clients with certain values? Would it be impossible? Why or why not? What should you do in problem cases?

4. Find ways to use person-centered concepts in your non-therapeutic personal and professional relationships. Take notes in a journal and share with others how these efforts influenced those relationships.

## QUESTIONS FOR STUDY AND DISCUSSION

1. Which Rogerian concepts most impact the development of the counseling profession overall and what has been that impact?

2. Some theoretical approaches are very different from person-centered. Which approaches are most different, what are those differences, and how do they influence work with clients?

3. How can person-centered theory be applied to teaching, parenting, and non-therapeutic personal or professional relationships?

4. How well does your belief system match your actions in everyday life as well as in counseling? What are the ways in which your beliefs and actions match and don't match those necessary for fully implementing a person-centered approach in counseling and everyday life.

## SUGGESTED READINGS

Boy, A., & Pine, G. (1990). *A person-centered foundation for counseling and psychotherapy*. Springfield, IL: Charles C Thomas.

Brazier, D. (Ed.) (1993). *Beyond Carl Rogers: Toward a psychotherapy for the 21st century*. London: Constable and Company Limited.

Farber, B. A., Brink, D. C., & Raskin, P. M. (Eds.) (1996). *The psychotherapy of Carl Rogers: Cases and Commentary*. New York: The Guilford Press.

Rogers, C. (1942). *Counseling and psychotherapy*. Boston: Houghton Mifflin.

Rogers, C. (1951). *Client-centered therapy*. Boston: Houghton Mifflin.

Rogers, C. (1959). A theory of therapy, personality, and interpersonal relationships, as developed in the client-centered framework. In S. Koch (Ed.), *Psychology: A study of a science*. New York: McGraw-Hill.

Rogers, C. (1961). *On becoming a person: A therapist's view of psychotherapy*. Boston: Houghton Mifflin.

Rogers, C. (Ed.). (1967). *The therapeutic relationship and its impact: A study of psychotherapy with schizophrenics*. Madison: University of Wisconsin Press.

Rogers, C. (1970). *Carl Rogers on encounter groups*. New York: Harper & Row.

Rogers, C. (1986). Carl Rogers on the development of the person-centered approach. *Person-centered Review, 1*(3), 257–259.

Rogers, C. (1987a). Inside the world of the Soviet professional. *Counseling and Values, 32*(1), 47–66.

Rogers, C. (1987b). Steps toward peace, 1948–1986: Tension reduction in theory and practice. *Counseling and Values, 32*(1), 12–16.

Rogers, C., & Dymond, R. (1954). *Psychotherapy and personality change*. Chicago: University of Chicago Press.

Rogers, C., & Sanford, R. (1987b). Reflections on our South African experience. *Counseling and Values, 32*(1), 17–20.

Watson, N. (1984). The empirical status of Rogers' hypotheses of the necessary and sufficient conditions for effective psychotherapy. In R. F. Levant & J. M. Shlien (Eds.), *Client-centered therapy and the person-centered approach: New directions in theory, research, and practice* (pp. 17-40). New York: Praeger.

## CHAPTER POST-INVENTORY

**INSTRUCTIONS: PLEASE ANSWER THE FOLLOWING QUESTIONS NOW THAT YOU HAVE COMPLETED READING THIS CHAPTER.**

T    F    1. The **PERSON-CENTERED THEORIST** views people as fully in charge of their lives and inherently motivated to improve themselves.

T    F    2. The **PHENOMENOLOGICAL PERSPECTIVE** refers to the uniqueness of each person's perspective.

T    F    3. The goal of **SELF-ACTUALIZATION** is achievement of perfection as a human.

T    F    4. Rogers believed that harmful thoughts and actions were reflections of a distorted view of self and the world.

T    F    5. One major limitation of person-centered theory is the lack of **EMPIRICAL RESEARCH** establishing its effectiveness.

T    F    6. A **POSITIVE VIEW OF HUMAN NATURE** is essential for the person-centered practitioner because of the major responsibilities clients are given in the direction, style, and content of counseling.

T    F    7. The **COUNSELOR'S ROLE** in person-centered counseling is to help the client **BECOME** good, constructive, and trustworthy.

T    F    8. Rogers believed that people use defensive thoughts and actions to protect themselves from **INCONGRUENCE**.

T    F    9. The **ESSENTIAL GOAL** for people experiencing psychological or sociological difficulties is to perceive their own positive nature more accurately and learn to use it more effectively in their everyday lives.

T    F    10. When individuals make judgments based upon expectations of others rather than their own best judgment, they are responding to perceived **CONDITIONS OF WORTH**.

T    F    11. **UNCONDITIONAL POSITIVE REGARD** should only be expressed when individuals have earned such regard with appropriate behaviors.

T    F    12. **PERSON-CENTERED THEORY** involves numerous techniques.

**T   F   13.** Empathic understanding refers only to the counselor's understanding of the client's world from the client's PHENOMENOLGICAL PERSPECTIVE.

**T   F   14.** The person-centered practitioner treats the client as an **EFFECTIVE HUMAN BEING** who will succeed regardless of the nature of his/her difficulties.

**T   F   15.** A major objective in person-centered therapy is to achieve **CONGRUENCE.**

**T   F   16.** Rogers believed that the **CORE CONDITIONS** (genuineness, unconditional positive regard, and empathic understanding) provide the necessary environment that allows individuals to implement their actualizing tendencies.

**T   F   17.** **INTERNAL LOCI OF CONTROL** develop when clients experience anxiety caused by internalizing "shoulds and oughts" from others running their lives.

**T   F   18.** **PERSON-CENTERED THEORY** is much more related to who a counselor is than to what a counselor does.

**T   F   19.** Being a **GENUINE** counselor means sharing every thought and feeling with a client.

**T   F   20.** **ACTIVE LISTENING** is the simple act of taking in information from the client.

# CHAPTER NINE
## _FEMINIST THEORY_

**CHAPTER PRE-INVENTORY**

**INSTRUCTIONS: PLEASE ANSWER THE FOLLOWING QUESTIONS BEFORE YOU READ THIS CHAPTER:**

T   F     1. **FEMINIST THEORY** seeks to adjust the inequality that exists between women and men by replacing our patriarchal society with matriarchy.

T   F     2. Feminist therapy strives to **EMPOWER WOMEN'S** life choices based on personal skills and interests, rather than on stereotypical gender roles.

T   F     3. Feminist counselors and therapists believe that traditional psychotherapies are flawed because of their **ANDROCENTRIC BIASES**.

T   F     4. Carol Gilligan defines **RESISTANCE** in adolescent girls as a phase in which girls dissociate from their authentic selves in order to adapt to society's image of how a "good" girl should behave.

T   F     5. One **FEMINIST PRINCIPLE** is the belief that the counselor or therapist and the client should establish a teacher/student therapeutic relationship.

T   F     6. In feminist theory, women's problems are mainly **INTRAPSYCHIC CONFLICTS**; therefore, they need help learning to better adapt to society.

T   F     7. **PLURALISM** is a feminist principle that celebrates the **SOCIOCULTURAL DIFFERENCES** among women, as well as the differences between women and men, acknowledging that these differences are all equally valuable.

T   F     8. Frequent counselor or therapist **SELF-DISCLOSURE** is necessary in feminist therapy.

T   F     9. In feminist therapy, **CHANGE** must be more than the awareness of oppression, it must involve activity to end the oppression.

T   F    10. One reason why many women have a **NEGATIVE BODY IMAGE** problem is that society places too much emphasis on a belief that there should be an "ideal" body size.

T   F    11. Some women develop **AVOIDANCE BARRIERS** in order to escape the embarrassment they feel about their bodies.

**T   F   12.** According to the DSM-IV, **WOMEN SUFFER FROM DEPRESSION** five times the rate of men.

**T   F   13.** Lesbians who are **COMING OUT** may need the help of a feminist counselor or therapist in weighing the benefits and the risks in order to decide if this action is appropriate.

**T   F   14.** The **MAIN STRESSORS** for most single-parent mothers are financial difficulties.

**T   F   15.** Feminist counselors and therapists have been **UNSUCCESSFUL** in their treatment of male clients.

**T   F   16.** By using an **AFROCENTRIC** model in feminist therapy, the counselor or therapist would focus on individualistic solutions for the client's presenting problem rather than community-oriented solutions.

**T   F   17.** When working with a battered woman client, **DEEP MUSCLE RELAXATION TECHNIQUES** can be used to help her become less **HYPERVIGILANT** about her environment.

**T   F   18.** Some **FEMINIST SCHOLARS** are examining ways to incorporate a more multicultural and diverse perspective that addresses minority women in feminist therapy theory.

**T   F   19.** After years of **BORROWING TRADITIONAL PSYCHOTHERAPIES**, feminist therapy has finally completed the development of its own unified theory.

**T   F   20.** There are **SEVERAL UNIVERSITIES** in the United States that offer doctoral programs in feminist therapy theory.

# CHAPTER 9 OUTLINE

**CHAPTER NINE**
**Feminist Theory**

I. **BACKGROUND**
   A. The Evolution of Feminist Therapy Theory
   B. Psychoanalytic Theory
   C. Object Relations Theory
   D. Jungian Theory
   E. Cognitive-Behavioral Theory
   F. Family Systems Theory

II. **HUMAN NATURE: A DEVELOPMENTAL PERSPECTIVE**
   A. Reframing Resistance
   B. The Authentic Self Versus the Inauthentic Self
   C. The Sexual Division of Labor
   D. The Quality of Connectedness
   E. Separation Versus Connection
   F. The Self-in-Relation
   G. Listening to Women's Stories at Mid-life

III. **MAJOR CONSTRUCTS**

IV. **APPLICATIONS**
   A. Overview
   B. Goals of Counseling and Psychotherapy
   C. The Process of Change
   D. Intervention Strategies
      1. Body Image
      2. Treatment of Depression in Women's Groups
      3. Lesbians: The Process of Coming Out
      4. Single-Parent Mothers and Stress
      5. Feminist Therapy With Men
      6. Issues for African American Women
      7. Working With Battered Women

V. **EVALUATION**
   A. Overview
   B. Supporting research
   C. Limitations

VI. **THE CASE STUDY OF MARIA: A FEMINIST APPROACH**
   A. Diagnosis
   B. Treatment Plan

VII. **REFERENCES**

## CHAPTER OVERVIEW

This chapter examines some of the misconceptions regarding the definition of feminism and the understanding of feminist therapy, and it looks at how feminist therapy theory has evolved over time. Problems with applying the male model of mental health to women are revealed in the traditional psychotherapies, and new feminist theories of female psychological development are described.

The literature surveyed indicates that most feminist scholars choose a specific women's issue and then apply intervention strategies using a feminist gender-political analysis of the problem.

Although much research is being done to develop a unified theory of feminist therapy, little feminist theory is being taught at the masters or doctoral levels at most universities. Study in this area tends to be done independently or through elective classes.

## KEY TERMS

National Organization for Women
Reframing
Intrapsychic conflicts
Object relations
Anima
Fusion
Complementary
Authentic selves
Lookism
Missing discourse of desire
Connectedness
Morality of responsibility
Egalitarian relationship
Feminist Therapy Institute
Boundaries
Sociocultural differences
"The personal is political"
Empowerment
Avoidance behaviors
"Coming out"
Culturally reinforced behavior
Deep muscle relaxation techniques
Feminist Therapy Institute's Ethical Code
APA Task Force on Sex Bias and
Sex-Role Stereotyping in Psychotherapy

Consciousness-raising groups
Androcentric bias
Dichotomous sex-role standards
Sociocultural factors
Animus
Reciprocity
Conceptual affirmative action
Resistance
Capitalism
Sexual division of labor
Morality of justice
Self-in relation theory
Ethical issues
Ethical standards
Pluralistic
Self-disclosure
Self-actualization
Negative body image
Assertiveness training
Black matriarchy
Hypervigilance
Hypnosis
Disidentification
Guided imagery
Feminist therapy

# Key People

Mary Ann Dutton-Douglas
Albert Ellis
Judd Marmor
Jo Romaniello
Betty Carter
Olga Silverstein
Mary Pipher
Michelle Fine
Jean Baker Miller
Judith Jordan
Mary Gergen
Mary Ballou
Mary Nomme Russell
Elayne A. Saltzberg
Lily McNair
Ellyn Kaschak
Broverman, Broverman Clarkson, Rosencrantz, & Vogel

Lenore E. A. Walker
Judith Lazerson
Phyllis Chesler
Marianne Walters
Peggy Papp
Carol Gilligan
Deborah Tolman
Nancy Chodorow
Lawrence Kohlberg
Janet Surrey
Laura S. Brown
Susan Sturdivant
Debra S. Srebnik
Jill Richard
Patricia Faunce
Ann Peterson

## CLASSROOM EXERCISES TO ENHANCE INSTRUCTION AND STUDENT LEARNING

1. Before reading chapter nine, ask students to write down their definition of "feminism" and their assumption of what they think feminist therapy entails. Collect what they have written. After reading the chapter, students will complete the same exercise. Then compare answers written both before and after reading the chapter and note any changes. Compile the results on the black board for comparison amongst the group.

2. Select volunteers to play the roles of counselor/therapist and client. Volunteers will demonstrate the use of the feminist therapy principles through role play. Discuss the results of the role play with the class.

3. Examine the students' viewpoints toward homosexuality in general and lesbianism specifically. Discuss gay stereotypes and homophobia and the related misconceptions about homosexuality. Discuss the climate of hate which surrounds the lesbian life style. Role play a "coming out" scene where the lesbian (or gay man) reveals her (his) homosexuality to friends and family members. Discuss the related emotions of both sides.

4. Divide the class into three groups. Each group will discuss the societal pressure faced by the individual in each of these situations:

a. A client with bulimia or anorexia nervosa.
b. A displaced home maker.
c. A college date rape victim.

Discuss feminist intervention strategies that might apply to the oppressed person, then share these with the class. Develop a matrix of possible strategies.

## INDIVIDUAL EXERCISES TO ENHANCE THE STUDENTS' LEARNING

1. Research a different women's issue than those listed in the book (e.g. anger, eating disorders, etc.). What intervention strategies are suggested? Which of the principles of feminist therapy are present in the text?

2. Interview a feminist therapist and discuss her educational background and training. Find out what opportunities exist in your area for feminist therapy training.

3. Prepare a collage of mediated body images from fashion magazines and compare the collage to actual body sizes and shapes. Identify how the mediated body images portray the body unrealistically, discuss how this unrealistic portrayal could cause problems in self-esteem.

## QUESTIONS FOR STUDY AND DISCUSSION

1. How does feminist therapy deal with the treatment of:
   a. Body Image
   b. Single Mothers and Stress
   c. Depression in Women

2. Create a time line charting the development of feminist therapy. Compare it to the development of a traditional therapy.

3. What are beliefs that underlie all of feminist therapy?

4. Compare and contrast the principles of feminist therapy with the major constructs of other more traditional psychotherapies, such as Adlerian theory, Person-Centered theory, or Existential theory. How are they different? What similarities do they share?

## SUGGESTED READINGS

Anderson, L., & Gold, K. (1994). I know what it means but it's not how I feel: The construction survivor identity in feminist counseling practice. *Women & Therapy*, 15 (2), 5-17.

Boyd-Franklin, N. (1991). Recurrent themes in the treatment of African-American in group psychotherapy. *Women & Therapy*, 11 (2), 25-40.

Caplan, P. J. (1992). Driving us crazy: How oppression damages women's mental health and what we can do about it. *Women & Therapy*, 12 (3), 5-28.

Comas-Diaz, L. (1987). Feminist therapy with Hispanic/ Latina women: Myth or reality? *Women & Therapy*, 6 (4), 39-61.

Goodrich, T. J., Rampage, C., Ellman, B., & Halstead, K. (1988). *Feminist family therapy.* NewYork, NY: W. W. Norton.

Luepnitz, D. A. (1988). *The family interpreted: psychoanalysis, feminism, and family therapy.* New York: Basic.

Myers, L. J. (1987). A therapeutic model for transcending oppression: A Black feminist perspective. *Women & Therapy*, 5 (4) 39-49.

Nadelson, C. C., & Notman, M. T. (1986). Psychotherapy and women: Changing issues. *Current Psychiatric Therapies*, 23, 13-25.

Robbins, J. H., & Siegel, R. J. (Eds.). (1985). *Women changing therapy: New assessments, values and strategies in feminist therapy.* New York: Harrington Park Press.

Rose, S. (1991). The contribution of Alice Miller to feminist therapy and theory. *Women & therapy*, 11 (2), 41-52.

Skodra, E. E. (1992). Ethnic/ immigrant women and psychotherapy: The issue of empowerment. *Women & Therapy*, 13 (4), 81-98.

# CHAPTER POST-INVENTORY

**INSTRUCTIONS: PLEASE ANSWER THE FOLLOWING QUESTIONS NOW THAT YOU HAVE COMPLETED READING THIS CHAPTER.**

T   F     1. **FEMINIST THEORY** seeks to adjust the inequality that exists between women and men by replacing our patriarchal society with matriarchy.

T   F     2. Feminist therapy strives to **EMPOWER WOMEN'S** life choices based on personal skills and interests, rather than on stereotypical gender roles.

T   F     3. Feminist counselors and therapists believe that traditional psychotherapies are flawed because of their **ANDROCENTRIC BIASES**.

T   F     4. Carol Gilligan defines **RESISTANCE** in adolescent girls as a phase in which girls dissociate from their authentic selves in order to adapt to society's image of how a "good" girl should behave.

T   F     5. One **FEMINIST PRINCIPLE** is the belief that the counselor or therapist and the client should establish a teacher/student therapeutic relationship.

T   F     6. In feminist theory, women's problems are mainly **INTRAPSYCHIC CONFLICTS**; therefore, they need help learning to better adapt to society.

T   F     7. **PLURALISM** is a feminist principle that celebrates the **SOCIOCULTURAL DIFFERENCES** among women, as well as the differences between women and men, acknowledging that these differences are all equally valuable.

T   F     8. Frequent counselor or therapist **SELF-DISCLOSURE** is necessary in feminist therapy.

T   F     9. In feminist therapy, **CHANGE** must be more than the awareness of oppression, it must involve activity to end the oppression.

T   F    10. One reason why many women have a **NEGATIVE BODY IMAGE** problem is that society places too much emphasis on a belief that there should be an "ideal" body size.

T   F    11. Some women develop **AVOIDANCE BARRIERS** in order to escape the embarrassment they feel about their bodies.

T   F    12. According to the DSM-IV, **WOMEN SUFFER FROM DEPRESSION** five times the rate of men.

T  F  13. Lesbians who are **COMING OUT** may need the help of a feminist counselor or therapist in weighing the benefits and the risks in order to decide if this action is appropriate.

T  F  14. The **MAIN STRESSORS** for most single-parent mothers are financial difficulties.

T  F  15. Feminist counselors and therapists have been **UNSUCCESSFUL** in their treatment of male clients.

T  F  16. By using an **AFROCENTRIC** model in feminist therapy, the counselor or therapist would focus on individualistic solutions for the client's presenting problem rather than community-oriented solutions.

T  F  17. When working with a battered woman client, **DEEP MUSCLE RELAXATION TECHNIQUES** can be used to help her become less **HYPERVIGILANT** about her environment.

T  F  18. Some **FEMINIST SCHOLARS** are examining ways to incorporate a more multicultural and diverse perspective that addresses minority women in feminist therapy theory.

T  F  19. After years of **BORROWING** traditional psychotherapies, feminist therapy has finally completed the development of its own unified theory.

T  F  20. There are **SEVERAL UNIVERSITIES** in the United States that offer doctoral programs in feminist therapy theory.

# NOTES

# CHAPTER TEN
## *GESTALT THERAPY*

**CHAPTER PRE-INVENTORY**

**INSTRUCTIONS: PLEASE ANSWER THE FOLLOWING QUESTIONS BEFORE YOU READ THIS CHAPTER:**

T    F    1. **MARTIN SHEPHERD** was Perls' biographer.

T    F    2. Perls asked clients to focus on **WHY** they behaved in certain ways.

T    F    3. Perls believed that the **CLICHE** layer of neurosis was one of **NON CONTACT** with others.

T    F    4. At one point in time, Perls and his wife **LAURA** relocated to **JOHANNES-BURG**, South Africa.

T    F    5. Perls disagreed with **KURT LEWIN'S** view of human nature.

T    F    6. Perls was seen by his contemporaries as a **CONSUMMATE ACTOR**.

T    F    7. Gestaltists use **DREAMWORK** to help clients understand their past.

T    F    8. The application of **DIALOGUE** is a unique contribution of Gestalt counseling and therapy.

T    F    9. Much has been done to extend Perls' individual approach to group work..

T    F    10. The **EMPTY OR TWO CHAIR** technique is a well-known intervention associated with Gestalt counseling and psychotherapy.

T    F    11. Gestalt counseling and psychotherapy is based on a **REDUCTIONISTIC** view of human nature.

T    F    12. **HOLISM/FIELD THEORY** and **SELF-ACTUALIZATION** are all major constructs associated with Gestalt theory.

T    F    13. One of the goals of Gestalt counseling and psychotherapy is providing an atmosphere that invites **CONTACT** between client and therapist.

**T   F**     14. The change process in Gestalt counseling and psychotherapy involves the client working through the **CLICHE, PHONY, IMPASSE, IMPLOSIVE** and **EXPLODING** layers of neurosis.

**T   F**     15. Gestalt interventions are usually labeled as "**EXPERIMENTS**".

**T   F**     16. One of the **LIMITATIONS** relating to Gestalt counseling and psychotherapy has little to do with Perls but with the theory itself.

**T   F**     17. Gestalt theory is rooted in **EXISTENTIALISM** and **PHENOMENOLOGY.**

**T   F**     18. **MAX WERTHEIMER** was one of the **"BERLIN THREE"** who influenced Perls' work.

**T   F**     19. **LAURA PERLS** contributed significantly to Gestalt counseling and psychotherapy.

**T   F**     20. **ENACTMENT** and **CONFRONTATION** enable the Gestaltist to involve the client in the change process.

# CHAPTER 10 OUTLINE

**CHAPTER TEN**
**Gestalt Theory**

## I. BACKGROUND
    A. Max Wertheimer
    B. Kurt Koffka
    C. Wolfgang Köhler
    D. Frederick (Fritz) Perls
    E. Laura Perls

## II. HUMAN NATURE: A DEVELOPMENTAL PERSPECTIVE

## III. MAJOR CONSTRUCTS
    A. Field Theory
        1. Phenomenological Field
        2. Differentiation and Contact
        3. Boundaries
        4. Dichotomies and Polarities
        5. Foreground and Background
    B. Awareness
    C. Responsibility
    D. Shoulds
    E. I–Thou, What and How, Here and Now

## IV. APPLICATIONS
    A. Overview
    B. Goals of Counseling and Psychotherapy
    C. The Process of Change
    D. Intervention Strategies
        1. Locating Feelings
        2. Confrontation and Enactment
        3. Empty-Chair or Two-Chair Strategy
        4. Dream Work
        5. Additional Strategies

## V. EVALUATION
    A. Overview
    B. Supporting Research
    C. Limitations

## VI. THE CASE OF MARIA: A GESTALT APPROACH
    A. Confrontation and Enactment
    B. Empty Chair

## VII. REFERENCES

## CHAPTER OVERVIEW

Gestalt counseling and psychotherapy is simultaneously simple and complex. Its simplicity is inherent in its evolutionary nature, making it easy to understand. The theory began as a philosophy, with Ehrenfels' work in 1890 and was expanded into psychology with the contributions of Wertheimer, Koffka, Köhler and Lewin.

Fritz Perls is credited with applying the Gestalt theory in therapy with the mentally ill. His followers in the United States have adopted his approach to work with clients who may not be mentally ill but who are temporarily dysfunctional and need assistance.

The complexity of Gestalt counseling and psychotherapy has to do with the fact that the student or practitioner must have mastered basic skills and simple interventions before moving on to interventions such as empty chair and dreamwork. The complexity of Gestalt counseling and psychotherapy is also escalated by the juxtaposition of its philosophy (existential) with its application (directive).

Within the framework of Gestalt theory the personhood of the counselor or therapist is extremely important. The Gestaltist needs to be balanced physically, mentally and emotionally before a therapeutic encounter in order to be fair to the client. A major strength of Gestalt counseling and psychotherapy is that the Gestaltist's role is to facilitate the client's "response-ability" to solve his or her own problems.

## KEY TERMS

Gestalt
Figure
Ground
Awareness through contact
Breathing and relaxation
Enactment and confrontation
Polarities
Dreamwork
Homework
The phony layer
Empty chair or two chair

The impasse layer
The exploding layer
Open-endedness
Unfinished business
Locating feelings
Identification and alienation
The now and the how
The cliche' layer

## KEY PEOPLE

E. Cadwallader
A. Dye
C. Ehrenfels
J. Enright
L. Greenberg
H. Hackney
G. Hartmann
M. Henle
H. Hormann
W. Kempler
K. Koffka
W. Köhler

A. Levitsky
K. Lewin
W. Passons
F. Perls
R. Hefferline
P. Goodman
E. Polster
M. Polster
M. Shepherd
J. Simkin
J. Swanson
M. Wertheimer
G. Yontef


## CLASSROOM EXERCISES TO ENHANCE INSTRUCTION AND STUDENT LEARNING

### Intervention #1: Gestalt Theory

1. Intervention/Condition: The Empty Chair.

2. Purpose of Intervention: The empty chair technique is employed to give the client an opportunity to: a) act in a way that he/she would like to with another person, and/ or b) rehearse a new or unfamiliar way of behaving. This technique spans the counseling/psychotherapy spectrum of concerns, problems or issues and can be used effectively with clients or any age--young children to the elderly.

3. Classroom Procedures:
    a. Introduce the technique to the entire class, allowing full discussion about the purpose of the technique.
    b. Demonstrate to the class the empty chair technique by playing both roles, client and counselor/therapist.
    c. Assuming that safety and trust are "givens" in the class, ask for a volunteer to suggest a real or hypothetical problem in her/his life.
    d. Remind class that Gestalt counseling/psychotherapy is process, rather than product oriented, so that a problem may not be resolved in a single set of interventions, but may simply encourage awareness in the client.
    e. Provide a certain amount of time to "set the stage" related to the introductory presenting issue. Class members are instructed to maintain some notes (but not extensive so as to distract their attention from the intervention experience).

f. Demonstrate the empty chair technique for 10-15 minutes by having the volunteer student, depending upon the problem issue, move into the chair whenever he/she wishes to address a third person, or whenever she/he is attempting a new or unfamiliar behavior.

g. At an appropriate intervening time, not necessarily having achieved closure, stop the activity and discuss with the entire class both the purpose of the interactions and expected behavior (of the client).

h. After sufficient discussion, ask the volunteer client to give feedback to the class about the process.

4. Indications for Use: This is a valuable experience for class members because it can be used effectively with fairly minimal training in the activity and can be used for school children or adults.

5. Contraindications: It is important that the counseling/psychotherapy students have a solid understanding of the purpose of this technique. It may appear simple enough in demonstration, but the students must know the "why"of the techniques as well as the "how."

6. Source:
   Korb, M., Garell, J., & Van De Riet, V. (1989). *Gestalt Therapy: Practice and theory* (2nd ed.). New York: Pergamon Press.
   Thompson, C. L., & Rudolph, L. B. (1992). *Counseling children* (3rd ed.). Monterey, CA: Brooks/Cole

7. Additional Readings:
   Greenberg, L., & Webster, M. (1982). Resolving decisional conflict through Gestalt two chair dialogue: Relating process to outcome. *Journal of Counseling Psychology, 29*, 468-477.

## Intervention #2: Gestalt Theory

1. Intervention/Condition: Gestalt Experience Cycle.

2. Purpose: It is valuable for students of Gestalt to understand the beginning and completion of a Gestalt. While not a true "intervention" in the conventional sense, it demonstrates the principle of holism in an easily understood manner by students of Gestalt.

3. Classroom Procedures:
   a. Because of the several stages involved, students should be apprised that this activity may last for several class sessions.
   b. While a bit unorthodox, the instructor might ask for a group of eight volunteers, each of whom will "play" the role of a particular function in the experience cycle.
   c. The instructor explains (reviews) the stages of the Experience Cycle: 1) Emer-

gence of the Gestalt; 2) Sensation, arousal or emergence of a need for action; 3) Achieving awareness or attention; 4) Involvement or Mobilization of Energy; 5) Making contact or taking action; 6) Assimilation or rejection; 7) Satisfaction; fulfillment or understanding; and 8) Withdrawal or energy directed inward and finally the experience or Gestalt is complete.

d. The instructor elicits a problem, issue or concern, real or hypothetical, that can be incorporated into the Experience Cycle.

e. The instructor reminds the class that this activity could take two or three class sessions to complete, dependent upon the process.

f. The completion of the Gestalt from Stage 1 to Stage 7 may take from two to three hours. Class will keep track of emergence from stage to stage.

g. When the cycle is completed, class will separate into eight small groups with the student volunteer for each stage in the cycle leading the group. Each group will spend 15 minutes discussing factors that occurred in his/her stage.

h. The instructor will then complete the activity by eliciting feedback from each group in order to complete the cycle.

4. <u>Indications for Use</u>: This activity might be used effectively at the beginning of the study of Gestalt theory. The principle of holism/process orientation is important for students to grasp early in their exploration to avoid easy or simplified solutions.

5. <u>Contraindications</u>: Even at the beginning of the study of Gestalt, it is important for the students to have a thorough grasp of the Experience Cycle. This avoids any breakdown of stages or tangential thinking.

6. <u>Source</u>:
Korb, M., Garell, J., & Van De Riet, V. (1989). *Gestalt therapy: Practice and theory* (2nd ed.). New York: Pergamon Press.

7. <u>Additional Readings</u>:
Aylward, J. (1988). A session with Cindy. *Gestalt Journal*, <u>111</u>, 51-62.
Brown, G. (1986). *The neurotic behavior of organizations*. Cleveland: Gestalt Institute of Cleveland Press.
Hendlin, S. (1987). Gestalt therapy: Aspects of evolving theory and practice. *Humanistic psychologist*, 15 (3), 184-196.

**Intervention #3: Gestalt Theory**

1. <u>Intervention/Condition</u>: Awareness training for elementary school classroom activity.

2. <u>Purpose</u>: Again, with the principle of holism that permeates Gestaltism the first stage of any Gestalt is to become aware of one's self (or internal awareness), aware of the outside world and aware of expressive feeling. In order for one to be an effective gestalt counselor/therapist, it is necessary for one to be in touch with self. This activity can be designed for children as clients in the counseling/therapy process.

3. Classroom Procedures:
   a. It is important to discuss the many creative ways in which awareness training can take place, i.e., through art, music, drama, journal writing, homework assignments and others. The method used will depend upon the creativity of the counselor/therapist.
   b. The instructor may use the class (in this case, drawings) as the client, thereby allowing them the full experience.
   c. Students are asked to play the roles of children for this activity, since it is so valuable for children.
   d. Students are asked to draw the things or people closest to them paying particular attention to themselves and their place in the drawing. Attention is also drawn to particular aspects of the personal appearance in the drawing and what the subject is feeling in the drawing.
   e. Next the students are directed to observe the environment surrounding the person in the drawing, elaborating on parts describing shapes, forms and colors.
   f. After a 30 minute experience involving both the drawing and the sharing of feelings in the drawings by students, the instructor will reconstruct the experience from a counseling or therapeutic mode, allowing the class members to be able to accompany a child through this experience, utilizing the classroom Gestalt guidance goals of external awareness and expressing feelings.
   g. In a more didactic way, the instructor will conclude by "walking" the students through a more detailed journey through the drawings, using their drawing examples.

4. Indications for Use: Gestalt experience activities such as the one described above are of much value when working involvement and verbal participation on the client's part. This activity is helpful particularly with reluctant or involuntary clients.

5. Contraindications: It is important that the counselor/therapist avoid, as can happen in Dream work-- another Gestalt technique, being trapped into interpretation rather than discussion about "here and now" feelings about the drawings.

6. Source:
   Oaklander, V. (1988). *Windows to our children*. Highland, NY: Center for Gestalt Development.
   Gibson, R., Mitchell, M., & Basile, S. (1993). *Counseling in the elementary school: A comprehensive approach*. Boston: Allyn and Bacon.


## INDIVIDUAL EXERCISES TO ENHANCE THE STUDENTS' LEARNING

1. Discuss the history of Gestalt counseling and psychotherapy including the influence of Wertheimer, Koffka and Köhler.

2. Describe Perls' view of human nature. What relationship do you see between Perls' view of human nature and the way Perls worked with clients.

3. Major constructs connected with Gestalt counseling and psychotherapy include experience and activity, figure-ground, here and now orientation, ego and boundaries and polarities. Briefly describe each of these constructs. How can you make user of each of these constructs in the process of working with clients within this theoretical framework?

4. Contributing to the process of change are Perls' five layers of neurosis that the client passes through in the process of change. What are these layers? How does experiencing each of these layers contribute to the change process?

## QUESTIONS FOR STUDY AND DISCUSSION

1. In what settings do you think Gestalt counseling and psychotherapy would most likely be applied: Why?

2. Who were the "Berlin Three" and how did each influence Perls' works?

3. How did the works of Kurt Lewin influence Perls' views?

4. Identify and discuss any three major constructs connected with Gestalt theory.

5. Discuss the goals of Gestalt counseling and psychotherapy.

6. What precepts influence the process of change in Gestalt counseling and psychotherapy?

7. Discuss Perls' five layers of neurosis.

8. Identify and discuss any three Gestalt interventions.

## SUGGESTED READINGS

Clarkson, P. and Mackeron, J. (1993). *Fritz Perls*. Newbury Park, CA: Sage

Dye, A., & Hackney, H. (1975). *Gestalt approaches to counseling*. Boston: Houghton Mifflin.

Freidman, N. (1993). Fritz Perls' 'layers' and the empty chair: A reconsideration. *The Gestalt Journal*, 16,2, 94-113.

Latner, J. (1992). Origin and development of Gestalt therapy. In E. C. Nevis (ed.) *Gestalt Therapy: Perspectives and Applications*. Cleveland, Ohio: Gestalt Institute of Cleveland Press.

Passons, W. (1975). *Gestalt approaches in counseling*. New York: Holt, Rinehart, & Winston.

Rock, I., & Palmer, S. (1990). *The legacy of Gestalt psychology*. Springfield, IL: Charles C. Thomas.

Rosenblatt, G. (1991). Interview with Laura Perls. *The Gestalt Journal*, 12,2, 16-27.

Stoehr, T. (1994). *Here, Now, Next: Paul Goodman and the Origins of Gestalt Therapy*. San Francisco: Jossey-Bass.

Wheeler, G. (1991). Gestalt reconsidered: A new approach to contact and resistance. New York: Gardner.

Wysong, J., & Rosenfeld, E. (1982). *An oral history of Gestalt therapy*. Highland, NY: The Gestalt Journal Press.

Yontef, G. (1993). *Awareness, Dialogue and Process: Essays on Gestalt Therapy*. Highland, N.Y.: The Gestalt Journal Press.

Zinker, J. (1978). *Creative process in Gestalt therapy*. New York: Vintage.

# CHAPTER POST-INVENTORY

**INSTRUCTIONS: PLEASE ANSWER THE FOLLOWING QUESTIONS NOW THAT YOU HAVE COMPLETED READING THIS CHAPTER:**

T  F   1. **MARTIN SHEPHERD** was Perls' biographer.

T  F   2. Perls asked clients to focus on **WHY** they behaved in certain ways.

T  F   3. Perls believed that the **CLICHE** layer of neurosis was one of **NON CONTACT** with others.

T  F   4. At one point in time, Perls and his wife **LAURA** relocated to **JOHANNES-BURG**, South Africa.

T  F   5. Perls disagreed with **KURT LEWIN'S** view of human nature.

T  F   6. Perls was seen by his contemporaries as a **CONSUMMATE ACTOR**.

T  F   7. Gestaltists used **DREAMWORK** to help clients understand their past.

T  F   8. The application of **DIALOGUE** is a unique contribution of Gestalt counseling and therapy.

T  F   9. Much has been done to extend Perls' individual approach to group work.

T  F   10. The **EMPTY OR TWO CHAIR** technique is a well-known intervention associated with Gestalt counseling and psychotherapy.

T  F   11. Gestalt counseling and psychotherapy is based on a **REDUCTIONISTIC** view of human nature.

T  F   12. **HOLISM/FIELD THEORY** and **SELF-ACTUALIZATION** are all major constructs associated with Gestalt theory.

T  F   13. One of the goals of Gestalt counseling and psychotherapy is providing an atmosphere that invites **CONTACT** between client and therapist.

T  F   14. The change process in Gestalt counseling and psychotherapy involves the client working through the **CLICHE, PHONY, IMPASSE, IMPLOSIVE** and **EXPLODING** layers of neurosis.

T  F   15. Gestalt interventions are usually labeled as "**EXPERIMENTS**".

**T    F**    16. One of the **LIMITATIONS** relating to Gestalt counseling and psychotherapy has little to do with Perls but with the theory itself..

**T    F**    17. Gestalt theory is rooted in **EXISTENTIALISM** and **PHENOMENOLOGY.**

**T    F**    18. **MAX WERTHEIMER** was one of the **"BERLIN THREE"** who influenced Perls' work.

**T    F**    19. **LAURA PERLS** contributed significantly to Gestalt counseling and psychotherapy.

**T    F**    20. **ENACTMENT** and **CONFRONTATION** enable the Gestaltist to involve the client in the change process.

# CHAPTER ELEVEN
## *COGNITIVE-BEHAVIORAL THEORIES*

**CHAPTER PRE-INVENTORY**

**INSTRUCTIONS: PLEASE ANSWER THE FOLLOWING QUESTIONS BEFORE YOU READ THIS CHAPTER.**

T   F   1. **"COGNITIVE-BEHAVIORAL"** is a term that reflects the primary importance of cognitions on helping human beings.

T   F   2. **BEHAVIORISM** was formed as a reaction against the Freudian emphasis on the unconscious as the subject matter of psychology. *+ introspection as method of investigation.*

T   F   3. **A STIMULUS-RESPONSE** relationship is essential to the classical behavioral paradigms.

T   F   4. **SYSTEMATIC DESENSITIZATION** is a behavioral approach used to treat depression.

T   F   5. **RATIONAL EMOTIVE BEHAVIOR THERAPY (REBT)** is based on the notion that human beings generate psychological disturbance by irrational emotions.

T   F   6. **COGNITIVE THERAPY**, developed by Aaron Beck, has been extremely influential in the treatment of depression.

T   F   7. **COGNITIVE INTERVENTIONS** attempt to produce change by influencing thinking.

T   F   8. **FUNCTIONAL ANALYSIS** refers to a statistical equation utilized to determine a client's presenting problem.

T   F   9. **COGNITIVE-BEHAVIORAL THEORY** views the relationship between the client and counselor as insignificant.

T   F   10. **BEHAVIORAL ASSESSMENTS** are completed at the onset of counseling to guide the direction of therapy.

T   F   11. **EMPIRICAL SUPPORT** refers to research that has demonstrated that a particular treatment is effective for a specific type of problem and client.

T (F)   12. **TRIPLE-RESPONSE MODE** refers to the client's visual, auditory, and tactile sensations.

(T) F   13. **SELF-EFFICACY** refers to an individual's expectations for personal success in performing specific behaviors.

(T) F   14. **POSITIVE REINFORCEMENT** is when positive feelings are increased following positive self-talk.

T (F)   15. **EXTINCTION** is used to describe the few "normal" people in our society.

(T) F   16. **SHAPING** is a behavioral intervention used to gradually increase the quality of a behavior.

T (F)   17. **STIMULUS CONTROL** is used to describe a method of controlling others in the environment around the client.

(T) F   18. **ALL-OR-NOTHING THINKING** is characterized by assuming that things are either 100% perfect or absolutely terrible.

(T) F   19. **THOUGHT STOPPING** is a procedure designed to interfere with thoughts that run through a client's mind and make it difficult to change behavior.

(T) F   20. **POSITIVE SELF-STATEMENTS** refers to the client's self-talk concerning his/her progress in therapy.

# CHAPTER 11 OUTLINE

## CHAPTER ELEVEN
## Cognitive-Behavioral Theories

I. **BACKGROUND**
   A. Watson and the Beginnings of Behavior Theory
   B. Skinner and Operant Conditioning
   C. Wolpe and Systematic Desensitization
   D. A Brief History of Cognitive Therapy

*Ellis – REBT* *language has a bearing.*
*Beck –* *faulty thinking → disturbed*
*consciousness – faulty learning*

II. **HUMAN NATURE: A DEVELOPMENTAL PERSPECTIVE** *Reality vs fantasy*

III. **MAJOR CONSTRUCTS**
   A. The Importance of Cognitions  *mediate Behaviors + Experience.*
   B. The Importance of Learning
   C. The Importance of Operational Definitions and Functional Analysis *of Antecedents + Consequences.*
   D. The Importance of Therapeutic Empathy

IV. **APPLICATIONS** *Δ Behaviors/Δ Cognitions  Directive, Structured, goal Directed, Time Ltd, Collaborative*
   A. Overview  *Home work, skills practice, problem solving Ability.*
   B. Goals of Counseling and Psychotherapy: Beginning With Assessment
   C. The Process of Change
      1. Self-Efficacy
      2. Does Changing Beliefs Lead to Change in Behavior?
   D. Intervention Strategies
      1. Behavioral Interventions
      2. Cognitive Interventions  *Dep*
      3. Cognitive-Behavioral Interventions
         a. Beck's Cognitive Therapy  *Depression*
         b. Ellis's Rational-Emotive Behavior Therapy
         c. Meichenbaum's Self Instructional Training and Stress Inoculation Training  *Anxiety.*

V. **EVALUATION**
   A. Overview
   B. Supporting Research
      1. Beck's Cognitive Therapy for Depression
      2. Meichenbaum's Self-Instructional Training and Stress Inoculation Training for Anxiety Disorders
   C. Limitations

VI. **THE CASE OF MARIA: A COGNITIVE-BEHAVIORAL APPROACH**

VII. **REFERENCES**

## CHAPTER OVERVIEW

Cognitive-behavioral theories are best conceptualized as a general category of theories, or a set of related theories, which have evolved from the theoretical writings, clinical experiences, and empirical studies of behavioral and cognitively oriented psychologists. There is no single definition of cognitive-behavioral theory. The individual theories are tied together by common assumptions, techniques and research strategies, but maintain a diversity of views about the role cognitions play in behavior change. The hyphenated term "cognitive-behavioral" reflects the importance of both behavioral and cognitive approaches to understanding and helping human beings. The hyphen brings together behavioral and cognitive theoretical views, each with its own theoretical assumptions and intervention strategies.

Cognitive-behavioral interventions target both cognitive and behavioral problems using a full integration of cognitive and behavioral strategies. Cognitive-behavioral research is based on observed changes in behavior and cognition with methodological rigor. Cognitive-behavioral theories provide great flexibility in treatment targets and interventions, sharing a fundamental emphasis on the importance of cognitive workings and private events as mediators of behavior change. Behavioral assessment, operating in the "triple response mode", provides a conceptual model of the functional relationships between thoughts, behaviors, and feelings and provides the necessary background for clinicians and researchers to implement and evaluate intervention strategies. Cognitive-behavioral theories and counseling interventions are currently highly influential. There are many different cognitive-behavioral intervention techniques and the number is likely to grow as the theories continue to be developed and tested for effectiveness with a variety of psychological problems.

## KEY TERMS

Cognitive-Behavioral

Cognitive Therapy

Rational Emotive Behavioral Therapy (REBT)

Stress Inoculation Training

Self-Instruction Training (SIT)

Classical Conditioning

Behaviorism

Operant Conditioning

Systematic Desensitization

Tabula Rosa

functional Analysis

Behavioral Assessment

Self-efficacy Theory

Positive Reinforcement

Extinction

Shaping

Stimulus Control

All-or-nothing Thinking

Disqualifying the Positive

Catastrophizing

Thought Stopping

Positive Self-Statements

Irrational Thinking

Operational Definitions

Therapeutic Empathy

Empirical Support

Reinforcement

Negative Reinforcement

## KEY PEOPLE

A. Beck

D. Meichenbaum

Pavlov

K. Wolpe

A. Ellis

J. Watson

B. Skinner

A. Bandura

## CLASSROOM EXERCISES TO ENHANCE INSTRUCTION AND STUDENT LEARNING

1.  Divide the class into two groups, asking one group to represent the cognitive therapy approach and the other group to represent the behavioral therapy approach to counseling. Debate the usefulness of each approach.

2.  Divide the class into four groups, and assign each group a specific presenting problem (e.g. depression due to divorce, test anxiety, poor self-esteem, fear of heights). Determine which cognitive-behavioral approach would work best. Brainstorm possible cognitive-behavioral excesses and deficits for each presenting problem, as well as cognitive-behavioral interventions for each.

3.  Discuss the ways that the following behaviors can be learned:

    (A) self-care          (E) healthy eating
    (B) assertiveness      (F) exercising
    (C) anger control      (G) skills
    (D) honest communication

4.  Invite a therapist that uses a cognitive-behavioral approach to counseling to demonstrate a role play in your class.

5.  Show video tapes of REBT and another cognitive-behavioral approach to therapy. Compare and contrast the approaches.

## INDIVIDUAL EXERCISES TO ENHANCE STUDENTS' LEARNING

1.  What do you see as the major differences between the "behavioral" and "cognitive-behavioral" theoretical approaches to theory?

2.  According to the author, "cognitive behavioral" theory developed from the "behavioral" approach. What do you see as the factors which influenced this development?

3.  What do you see as the major differences between the "cognitive behavioral" approaches of Aaron Beck and Donald Meichenbaum?

4. Where does the counselor-client relationship fit into the "cognitive-behavioral" approach? How important is this relationship when compared to the "person-centered" approach?

## QUESTIONS FOR STUDY AND DISCUSSION

1. Review the various cognitive-behavioral approaches listed in this chapter. Discuss the similarities and differences between the approaches. Identify the variables that contribute to both the unique aspects of these groups and their commonalities.

2. Review various behavioral interventions (extinction, reinforcement, punishment, shaping, and stimulus control). Identify daily events/interactions where such interventions occur or may occur.

3. Review the types of cognitive distortions (all-or-nothing thinking, disqualifying the positive, and catastrophizing); brainstorm 3-4 examples of each type of distortion. Review cognitive interventions (thought stopping and positive self-statements); apply the interventions to each example of cognitive distortions.

## SUGGESTED READINGS

Bandura, A. (1977). Self-Efficacy: Toward a unifying theory of behavior change. *Psychological Review* 84, 191-215.

Beck, A. T., Freeman, A., & Associates. (1990). *Cognitive therapy of personality disorders*. New York: Guilford Press.

Beck, A. T., Rush, A. J., Shaw, B. F., & Emery, G. (1979). *Cognitive therapy of depression*. New York: Guilford Press.

Beck, A. T., Wright, F. D., Newman, C. F., & Liese, B. S. (1993). *Cognitive therapy of substance abuse*. New York: Guilford Press.

Ellis, A. (1962). *Reason and emotion in psychotherapy*. New York: Lyle Stuart Press.

Ellis, A. & Grieger, R. (1986). *Handbook of rational-emotive therapy*, Vol 2, New York: Springer Publishing Company.

Meichenbaum, D. (1977). *Cognitive behavior modification: An integrative approach*. New York: Plenum.

Meichenbaum, D. (1985). *Stress inoculation training*. New York: Pergamon Press.

# CHAPTER POST-INVENTORY

**INSTRUCTIONS: PLEASE ANSWER THE FOLLOWING QUESTIONS NOW THAT YOU HAVE COMPLETED READING THIS CHAPTER.**

T  F  1. **"COGNITIVE BEHAVIORAL"** is a term that reflects the primary importance of cognitions on helping human beings.

T  F  2. **BEHAVIORISM** was formed as a reaction against the Freudian emphasis on the unconscious as the subject matter of psychology.

T  F  3. **A STIMULUS-RESPONSE** relationship is essential to the classical behavioral paradigms.

T  F  4. **SENSITIVE DESENSITIZATION** is a behavioral approach used to treat depression.

T  F  5. **RATIONAL EMOTIVE BEHAVIOR THERAPY (REBT)** based on the notion that human beings generate psychological disturbance by irrational emotions.

T  F  6. **COGNITIVE THERAPY,** developed by Aaron Beck, has been extremely influential in the treatment of depression.

T  F  7. **COGNITIVE INTERVENTIONS** attempt to produce change by influencing thinking.

T  F  8. **FUNCTIONAL ANALYSIS** refers to a statistical equation utilized to determine a client's presenting problem.

T  F  9. **COGNITIVE-BEHAVIORAL THEORY** views the relationship between the client and counselor as insignificant.

T  F  10. **BEHAVIORAL ASSESSMENTS** are completed at the onset of counseling to guide the direction of therapy.

T  F  11. **EMPIRICAL SUPPORT** refers to research that has demonstrated that a particular treatment is effective for a specific type of problem and client.

T  F  12. **TRIPLE-RESPONSE MODE** refers to the client's visual, auditory, and tactile sensations.

T  F  13. **SELF-EFFICACY** refers to an individual's expectations for personal success in performing specific behaviors.

**T  F  14. POSITIVE REINFORCEMENT** is when positive feelings are increased following positive self-talk.

**T  F  15. EXTINCTION** is used to describe the few "normal" people in our society.

**T  F  16. SHAPING** is a behavioral intervention used to gradually increase the quality of a behavior.

**T  F  17. STIMULUS CONTROL** is used to describe a method of controlling others in the environment around the client.

**T  F  18. ALL-OR-NOTHING THINKING** is characterized by assuming that things are either 100% perfect or absolutely terrible.

**T  F  19. THOUGHT STOPPING** is a procedure designed to interfere with thoughts that run through a client's mind and make it difficult to change behavior.

**T  F  20. POSITIVE SELF-STATEMENTS** refers to the client's self-talk concerning his/her progress in therapy.

# CHAPTER TWELVE
## _REALITY THERAPY THEORY_

**CHAPTER PRE-INVENTORY**

**INSTRUCTIONS: PLEASE ANSWER THE FOLLOWING QUESTIONS BEFORE YOU READ THIS CHAPTER.**

**T    F**    1. The theoretical basis for reality therapy is called **CHOICE THEORY**.

**T    F**    2. The name of the theory was **CHANGED TO EMPHASIZE** that human beings are not free but can learn to become free.

**T    F**    3. In choice theory people are said to be **INTERNALLY MOTIVATED**.

**T    F**    4. There are five basic **UNIVERSAL SOURCES** of human motivation.

**T    F**    5. The **BASIC MOTIVATORS** are learned not innate.

**T    F**    6. These **SOURCES OF BEHAVIOR** are survival, belonging, power, freedom and fun.

**T    F**    7. **POWER IMPLIES** not domination of others, but rather, an inner sense of achievement.

**T    F**    8. The specific collection of **DESIRES AND WANTS** is called the "quality world."

**T    F**    9. In choice theory **HUMAN BEHAVIOR IS COMPOSED OF** action, thinking, feelings and physiology.

**T    F**    10. **FEELINGS** are more easily changed than any other component of the behavioral system.

**T    F**    11. **THINKING** is seen as the cause of all actions.

**T    F**    12. **ONE PART** of the behavioral system does not cause any other part of it.

**T    F**    13. In practicing reality therapy, **A WARM HUMAN RELATIONSHIP** is unnecessary.

**T    F**    14. The environment or atmosphere serves as the **FOUNDATION** for effective interventions.

T    F      15. The counselor must be part of the **CLIENT'S QUALITY WORLD** if counseling is to succeed.

T    F      16. **FEELINGS** are never discussed nor dealt with in reality therapy.

T    F      17. In the **ACTUAL DIALOGUE** between client and counselor the emphasis is on actions.

T    F      18. **SELF-EVALUATION** is the cornerstone of reality therapy. There is no change without unless it occurs.

T    F      19. The self-evaluation by clients **INCLUDES JUDGEMENTS** about the effectiveness of their behavior and the attainability of their wants.

T    F      20. Though the plan is widely associated with the practice of reality therapy, it is **NOT AS IMPORTANT** to each session as self-evaluation.

# CHAPTER 12 OUTLINE

**CHAPTER TWELVE**
**Reality Therapy Theory**

I.   **BACKGROUND**

II.  **HUMAN NATURE:  A DEVELOPMENTAL PERSPECTIVE**
    A. Development of Mental Health
       1. Regressive Stages
       2. Positive Stages

III. **MAJOR CONSTRUCTS**

IV.  **APPLICATIONS**
    A. Overview
    B. Goals of Counseling and Psychotherapy
    C. The Process of Change
       1. Present Orientation
       2. Emphasis on Choice
       3. Control of Action
       4. Importance of Relationship
       5. Metacommunication

    D. Intervention Strategies
       1. Environment
          a. Use Attending Behaviors
          b. Suspend Judgment
          c. Do the Unexpected
          d. Use Humor
          e. Be Yourself
          f. Share Yourself
          g. Listen for Metaphors
          h. Listen for Themes
          I. Summarize and Focus
          j. Allow or Impose Consequences
          k. Allow Silence
          l. Be Ethical
          m. Be Redundant or Repetitious
          n. Create Suspense and Anticipation
          o. Establish Boundaries
       2. Procedures: The WDEP System
          a. Discussing Wants, Needs and Perceptions
          b. Sharing Wants and Perceptions
          c. Getting a Commitment to Counseling

## CHAPTER OVERVIEW

This chapter is a summary of reality therapy and its theoretical base, Choice Theory [formerly known as Control Theory]. Choice theory is based on the view of human beings as motivated by five innate human needs. These express themselves in specific wants which drive the behavioral system. Behavior impacts the external world so as to fulfill needs. Behavior is seen as a choice rather than determined by external stimuli or childhood conflicts.

The delivery system, reality therapy, is composed of two components: Environment and procedures. Establishing a friendly, warm relationship is the basis for further interventions. But empathy is not seen as sufficient to effect change.

The procedures are built on the environment and are summarized in the *W D E P* formulation. Each letter represents a cluster of ideas: W - Exploring wants, perceptions and level of commitment; D - Discussing four aspects of behavior - actions, thinking, feelings and even physiology; E - Assisting clients to evaluate their behavior, wants, level of commitment; P - Encouraging clients to make specific attainable plans.

Reality therapy is based on choice theory and empirical research. It has been used in schools, drug programs, mental health agencies, supervision, parenting and family relationships.


## KEY TERMS

Choice theory

Belonging

Power

Freedom

Quality world

Choices

Environment

Wants

Locus of control

Thinking, cognition

Self-Evaluation

SAMI$^2$C$^3$ planning

External controls

"External control psychology"

Power

Fun

Survival

Total behavior

Perceptions

Procedures

Level of commitment

Actions

Feelings

Control theory

External stimuli


## KEY PEOPLE

W. Glasser

R. Wubbolding

E. Ford

## CLASSROOM EXERCISES TO ENHANCE INSTRUCTION AND STUDENT LEARNING

1. Divide the class into groups of four and have them apply the needs to their own lives. Ask them to identify their own needs which are, overall, being fulfilled adequately on an ongoing basis. Then ask them to discuss needs which they believe could be more effectively satisfied.

2. Divide the class into triads or groups of four and ask them to discuss what they want in the following areas: job/career, school, friends, family, recreational life. Have them identify other areas to discuss relative to their needs.

3. In groups of three or four have them discuss behaviors which clients choose which are ineffective. How do clients give up and then choose negative symptoms? What do clients do when they give up? What do they do when they choose negative symptoms? How would they recognize these stages in their clients?

4. Divide the class into teams to have a debate. One group defends reality therapy, another defends psychoanalytic, REBT, or any other theory.

5. In triads students role play clients of their choosing. The counselor uses the *WDEP* system. The observers identify the needs of the client as well as the specific procedures used by the counselor.

## INDIVIDUAL EXERCISES TO ENHANCE THE STUDENTS' LEARNING

1. Identify your own needs and wants that are met by being a counselor.
   a. Is meeting your own needs as a counselor legitimate? Why? Why not?
   b. When is it inappropriate to meet your own needs? What are the relevant ethical considerations?

2. Interview professional counselors to determine their view of reality therapy.
   a. Do they understand reality therapy as it is explained in this chapter?
   b. From these interviews formulate a list of misconceptions about this method.

3. Watch video tapes of other counseling theories for comparison.
   a. How would you counsel the same client using the *WDEP* system?
   b. What client needs, both met and unmet, can you identify in the tapes?
   c. What do the clients want that they are not getting?

4. Investigate through library research how reality therapy is applied to:
   a. Multicultural counseling
   b. Family therapy
   c. Domestic violence
   d. Personal growth

5. How would you use the *WDEP* system in a consultation setting?
    a. To identify the client system
    b. To determine the client's wants
    c. To help clients evaluate their own behavior and plan for the future

## QUESTIONS FOR STUDY AND DISCUSSION

1. Compare reality therapy with Adlerian and REBT.

2. Why does reality therapy emphasize present behavior?

3. When does the reality therapist need to learn about past behaviors?

4  What are some adjustments in the use of reality therapy that need to be made in a multicultural setting?

5. How do you think elementary and secondary school teachers can use the *WDEP* system in their classrooms?

6. Can reality therapy be used only in a directive way or can it be used in a more non-directive or reflective way?

7. When are questions appropriate and inappropriate in the use of reality therapy?

## SUGGESTED READINGS

Glasser, W. (1986b). *Control theory-reality therapy workbook.* Los Angeles: Institute for Reality Therapy.
Glasser, W. (1998). *Choice theory.* New York: Harper Collins.
Wubbolding, R. (1988). *Using reality therapy.* New York: Harper & Row.
Wubbolding, R. (1990b). *Expanding reality therapy.* Cincinnati: Real World.
Wubbolding, R. (1991). *Understanding reality therapy.* New York: Harper Collins.

**CHAPTER POST-INVENTORY**

**INSTRUCTIONS: PLEASE ANSWER THE FOLLOWING QUESTIONS NOW THAT YOU HAVE COMPLETED READING THIS CHAPTER.**

T    F    1. The theoretical basis for reality therapy is called **CHOICE THEORY**.

T    F    2. The name of the theory was **CHANGED TO EMPHASIZE** that human beings are not free but can learn to become free.

T    F    3. In choice theory people are said to be **INTERNALLY MOTIVATED**.

T    F    4. There are five basic **UNIVERSAL SOURCES** of human motivation.

T    F    5. The **BASIC MOTIVATORS** are learned not innate.

T    F    6. These **SOURCES OF BEHAVIOR** are survival, belonging, power, freedom and fun.

T    F    7. **POWER IMPLIES** not domination of others, but rather, an inner sense of achievement.

T    F    8. The specific collection of **DESIRES AND WANTS** is called the "quality world."

T    F    9. In choice theory **HUMAN BEHAVIOR IS COMPOSED OF** action, thinking, feelings and physiology.

T    F    10. **FEELINGS** are more easily changed than any other component of the behavioral system.

T    F    11. **THINKING** is seen as the cause of all actions.

T    F    12. **ONE PART** of the behavioral system does not cause any other part of it.

T    F    13. In practicing reality therapy, **A WARM HUMAN RELATIONSHIP** is unnecessary.

T    F    14. The environment or atmosphere serves as the **FOUNDATION** for effective interventions.

T    F    15. The counselor must be part of the **CLIENT'S QUALITY WORLD** if counseling is to succeed.

T    F    16. **FEELINGS** are never discussed nor dealt with in reality therapy.

T    F    17. In the **ACTUAL DIALOGUE** between client and counselor the emphasis is on actions.

T    F    18. **SELF-EVALUATION** is the cornerstone of reality therapy. There is no change without unless it occurs.

T    F    19. The self-evaluation by clients **INCLUDES JUDGEMENTS** about the effectiveness of their behavior and the attainability of their wants.

T    F    20. Though the plan is widely associated with the practice of reality therapy, it is **NOT AS IMPORTANT** to each session as self-evaluation.

# NOTES

# CHAPTER THIRTEEN
## *FAMILY THEORY*

**CHAPTER PRE-INVENTORY**

**INSTRUCTIONS: PLEASE ANSWER THE FOLLOWING QUESTIONS BEFORE YOU READ THIS CHAPTER.**

T    F    1. Developmental stressors are least intense during the transition points of the **FAMILY LIFE CYCLE**.

T    F    2. Stressors in the **FAMILY LIFE SPIRAL** are passed across many generations.

T    F    3. **CENTRIPETAL PERIODS** in family life are marked by intense bonding and cohesion.

T    F    4. Centrifugal periods in family life indicate a **PATHOLOGIC CONDITION**.

T    F    5. A **GENOGRAM** is a culturally sensitive tool for understanding families.

T    F    6. **VIRGINIA SATIR** saw health as a closed system with good communication.

T    F    7. **VIRGINIA SATIR'S** communication game is humorous but is not a concrete tool for therapy.

T    F    8. In **A CONGRUENT MESSAGE** both the non-verbal and verbal messages match.

T    F    9. The **EXTERNALIZATION** of the problem in narrative family therapy is an indication of pathology.

T    F    10. Families use an **INTERTWINED FAMILY STORY** style to make meaning of circumstances.

T    F    11. **HOLONS** are partial units nested in whole units.

T    F    12. **HOMEOSTASIS** is the term used to describe a family system's tendency to maintain predictable interactional processes.

T    F    13. In family therapy, **"IP"** stands for "identified patient."

T    F    14. Cleveland, Ohio was the home base for the work of **MINUCHIN.**

**T  F  15. VIRGINIA SATIR** is a noted structural family therapist.

**T  F  16. STRATEGIC FAMILY THERAPY** is based, in part, on the ideas of Michel Foucault.

**T  F  17.** The term **"NONSPECIFIC FACTORS"** applies to those change-producing elements present in counseling regardless of theoretical orientation.

**T  F  18.** Third-party ratings of family competence **DO NOT PREDICT** family therapy outcome.

**T  F  19.** Ratings of working alliance **DO NOT PREDICT** family therapy outcome.

**T  F  20. SECOND ORDER CHANGE** leads to change in the basic structure of a family system.

**CHAPTER THIRTEEN**
**Family Theory**

I. **BACKGROUND**
    A. Why a Chapter on Family Theory?
    B. Definitions

II. **HUMAN NATURE: A DEVELOPMENTAL PERSPECTIVE**
    A. The Family Life Cycle
    B. The Family Life Spiral
        1. Centripetal Periods
        2. Centrifugal Periods
        3. The Family Merry-Go-Round
        4. Implications for Practice
    C. The Family Genogram

III. **MAJOR CONSTRUCTS**
    A. Theoretical Antecedents
        1. Bateson
        2. The Palo Alto Group
    B. Conjoint Theory
    C. Strategic Theory
    D. Structural Theory
    E. Transgenerational Theory
    F. Narrative Theory

IV. **APPLICATIONS**
    A. Overview
    B. Goals of Counseling and Psychotherapy
    C. The Process of Change
        1. First Order Change
        2. Second Order Change
    D. Intervention Strategies
        1. Specific Versus Nonspecific Factors
        2. The Family Interview

V. **EVALUATION**
    A. Overview
    B. Supporting Research
    C. Limitations

## CHAPTER OVERVIEW

Family therapy is a counseling approach that addresses the patterns of communication and relationship that connect people to each other and to their social and physical environments. This chapter can be divided into four main parts. First, the specialized terminology used by family therapists is defined to build the student's professional vocabulary. With such a vocabulary in place, the content of the chapter shifts to an overview of the history of family therapy theory. This overview includes theorists such as Bateson, Satir, Haley, Minuchin, Bowen, and White. The emphasis focuses on how these theorists differ from the dominant individual-based counseling models. The purpose here is to broaden the clinical reasoning skills of the student.

The third part of the chapter explores the clinical applications of the theorists discussed in the chapter. Concrete examples of the goals and change processes in family therapy are provided. The purpose here is to add to the clinical tool bag of the student.

The chapter ends with a case study of a multigenerational family. Each member of the family is suffering from either direct or vicarious Post Traumatic Stress Disorder (PTSD). To help the family, the counselors employed a strategic family therapy approach. Also, to enhance their therapeutic working alliance with this family, they blended this approach with the use of both narratives and art media.

## KEY TERMS

Family Life Cycle                          Family Life Spiral
Genogram                                   Symptomatic Double Bind
Differentiation                            Externalization
Second Order Change                        Nonspecific Factors

## KEY PEOPLE

Gregory Bateson                            Cloe Madanes
Jay Haley                                  Virginia Satir
Salvador Minuchin                          Murray Bowen
Michael White                              William Pinsof

## CLASSROOM EXERCISES TO ENHANCE INSTRUCTION AND STUDENT LEARNING

1. <u>Family of Origin Story Styles</u>. Divide the class in groups of four to five people. Have each person write down a story they remember from their own family of origin. Remind them to select a story they can read aloud in their group. Allow about 10 minutes for this writing process. Instruct the groups to review Roberts' (1995)

(1995) (text page 329) "six types of story styles." Each person reads his/her story aloud to the group. When this is completed, instruct the groups to debrief about the process. Allow at least 30 minutes for this discussion.

Regroup the class for a discussion. Ask the groups to report what happened during this process. Add any other class contributions to the board. Close with a class discussion of the power of family of origin stories in the training of counselors.

2. Family Story Styles and Art. Follow the instructions for the Family Story Styles exercise above just up until the stories have been written. Then introduce art materials of soft chalk pastels (box of 12 colors) on newsprint paper (18" x 24"). Tell the groups to draw colors, shapes, or symbols to portray their experience of the story they just wrote. Encourage spontaneity by having the students draw with their non-dominant hand. Allow about 15 minutes before stopping the drawing process.

   Follow this with a discussion about what memories, feelings, or thoughts emerged through the art process. Reconvene the whole class to consider how themes and images changed when written and when drawn. Conclude with a discussion of the power of art as a tool in family therapy work.

3. Family Communication. Break the class up into small groups of four or five students each. In these groups, compile a list of communication problems that can occur in families. Also, list those traits that describe positive family communication. Have each small group compare its list with the larger group. Which traits were mentioned most often? Allow 30 minutes for this exercise.

4. Walk the Talk. Before class, make a sign for each of the theories covered in the chapter (i.e. conjoint, strategic, structural, transgenerational, and narrative). Place the signs in different parts of the room. When class begins, have the students gather in the center of the room. Then, ask the students to move to the sign that best represents their family therapy theoretical orientation. Once the students have moved to the sign of their choice, direct them to sit down next to that sign. The small group at each sign makes a list of reasons why it chose that theoretical orientation. Compare and contrast the lists. Allow 45 minutes for this exercise.

## INDIVIDUAL EXERCISES TO ENHANCE STUDENTS' LEARNING

1. Based on the family communication theorists' understanding of incongruence, consider two examples of family situations where this type of miscommunication has occurred in your life. Scenarios to consider may include:
   a. Holiday dinners

b. Allocation of work around the house
  c. Use of the family car keys or money

2. Considering the narrative family therapy tool for externalizing problems, write down a brief story example of a problem you have in your own family life. Questions to answer for yourself afterward include:
  a. What other name can you call the problem so it is a separate entity from yourself?
  b. What would the newly named problem say to you about itself?
  a. How would the story be different using this externalization?

3. Review the discussion on centripetal and centrifugal families in the chapter. Which of these terms best describes your family-of-origin right at the present moment? What characteristics of your family suggest a centripetal or centrifugal label at this time?

4. Reread the definition of Family Projection Process in the first part of the chapter. Could any of the children in your family-of-origin fit the definition of IP? What characteristics best describe this child(ren)? What specifically was the IP(s) drawing attention away from?

## QUESTIONS FOR STUDY AND DISCUSSION

1. Identify the key components of Satir's communication game. Consider how this game might be applied to different client populations. For example, how would socioeconomic status or cultural heritage impact the game playing process? Conclude with a discussion of the cultural features of communication.

2. Review the section on narrative theory in the chapter including Table 13-1. Discuss the limitations and benefits of the narrative approach to family therapy (i.e. role of therapist, view of pathology, and techniques).

3. Reread the discussion on symptomatic double binds. To what extent is the double bind theory a "blame the victim" theory? What does the current professional literature on psychopathology say about double binds as a casual factor?

4. There exists strong evidence to suggest that working alliance is a powerful predictor of treatment outcome. Yet, many family therapy theorists suggest counselors employ directive and manipulative activities with counseling. Why? Also, do intentional, planned manipulations ever have a role in counseling?

## SUGGESTED READINGS

Carter, E. A., & McGoldrick, M. (1988). *The changing life cycle: A framework for family therapy.* New York: Gardner.

Lebow, J. L., & Gurman, A. S. (1995). Research assessing couple and family therapy. *Annual Review of Psychology,* 46, 25-57.

McGoldrick, M., & Gerson, R. (1985). *Genograms in family assessment.* New York: Norton.

Satir, V. M. *Conjoint family therapy.* Palo Alto, CA: Science and Behavior Books.

White, M., & Epston, D. (1990). *Narrative means to therapeutic ends.* New York: Norton.

## CHAPTER POST-INVENTORY

**INSTRUCTIONS: PLEASE ANSWER THE FOLLOWING QUESTIONS NOW THAT YOU HAVE COMPLETED READING THIS CHAPTER:**

T    F        1. Developmental stressors are least intense during the transition points of the **FAMILY LIFE CYCLE**.

T    F        2. Stressors in the **FAMILY LIFE SPIRAL** are passed across many generations.

T    F        3. **CENTRIPETAL PERIODS** in family life are marked by intense bonding and cohesion.

T    F        4. Centrifugal periods in family life indicate a **PATHOLOGIC CONDITION**.

T    F        5. A **GENOGRAM** is a culturally sensitive tool for understanding families.

T    F        6. **VIRGINIA SATIR** saw health as a closed system with good communication.

T    F        7. **VIRGINIA SATIR'S** communication game is humorous but is not a concrete tool for therapy.

T    F        8. In **A CONGRUENT MESSAGE** both the non-verbal and verbal messages match.

T    F        9. The **EXTERNALIZATION** of the problem in narrative family therapy is an indication of pathology.

T    F        10. Families use an **INTERTWINED FAMILY STORY** style to make meaning of circumstances.

T    F        11. **HOLONS** are partial units nested in whole units.

T    F        12. **HOMEOSTASIS** is the term used to describe a family system's tendency to maintain predictable interactional processes.

T    F        13. In family therapy, **"IP"** stands for "identified patient."

T    F        14. Cleveland, Ohio was the home base for the work of **MINUCHIN.**

T    F        15. **VIRGINIA SATIR** is a noted structural family therapist.

T    F        16. **STRATEGIC FAMILY THERAPY** is based, in part, on the ideas of Michel Foucault.

**T  F**    17. The term **"NONSPECIFIC FACTORS"** applies to those change-producing elements present in counseling regardless of theoretical orientation.

**T  F**    18. Third-party ratings of family competence **DO NOT PREDICT** family therapy outcome.

**T  F**    19. Ratings of working alliance **DO NOT PREDICT** family therapy outcome.

**T  F**    20. **SECOND ORDER CHANGE** leads to change in the basic structure of a family system.

# CHAPTER 14
## *BRIEF THEORY*

**CHAPTER PRE-INVENTORY**

**INSTRUCTIONS: PLEASE ANSWER THE FOLLOWING QUESTIONS BEFORE YOU READ THIS CHAPTER.**

T    F    1. Brief Counseling is represented by a small number of **UNIFORM THEORIES**.

T    F    2. **BRIEF AND LONG TERM COUNSELING** are two distinct and clearly delineated approaches to treatment.

T    F    3. **THE AVERAGE NUMBER OF SESSIONS** for clients receiving outpatient counseling is often reported as 6 with a mode of 1 session.

T    F    4. In addition to specific counseling interventions, several domains or "factors" such as the nature of the **THERAPY RELATIONSHIP** and **CLIENT RE-SOURCES** help predict client change.

T    F    5. **SYSTEMATIC TREATMENT SELECTION** is an attempt to develop an integrated, holistic approach to counselor decision making based on factors found to be most predictive of client change.

T    F    6. According to Systematic Treatment Selection theory, the inability of research to define specific **DECISION MAKING CRITERIA** for selecting appropriate counseling interventions is based on imprecise diagnostic systems and research-ers focusing on variables not deemed relevant by clinicians.

T    F    7. **COUNSELING RELATIONSHIP FACTORS** such as credibility, genuine-ness, and caring are definable and counselors can be trained to make conscious use of them.

T    F    8. Systematic Treatment Selection used for brief counseling interventions focuses on client diagnosis and rarely addresses **ENVIRONMENTAL FACTORS** that may cause distress.

T    F    9. Systematic Treatment Selection does not address **CLIENT SELECTION CRITERIA** for brief counseling.

T    F    10. Systematic Treatment Selection used for brief counseling emphasizes clinical wisdom over **PSYCHOTHERAPY OUTCOME RESEARCH**.

T   F     11. **SOCIAL CONSTRUCTIONIST PHILOSOPHY** contributed to the development of Brief Solution-Focused Therapy.

T   F     12. BSFT focuses on client strengths and may be considered to be a **MENTAL HEALTH RESOURCE MODEL**.

T   F     13. **MILTON ERICKSON** is an important figure in the development of brief psychotherapy.

T   F     14. **NARRATIVE THERAPY** and BSFT share some overlapping concepts concerning the way in which people interpret their experiences.

T   F     15. Clients' inherent **SELF CORRECTING TENDENCIES** are an important part of the change equation for BSFT.

T   F     16. Client diagnosis helps **BRIEF SOLUTION FOCUSED** therapists determine treatment goals.

T   F     17. Brief Solution Focused therapists see themselves as **EXPERTS** on their clients' difficulties and solutions.

T   F     18. In BSFT **CLIENT SELECTION CRITERIA** are clearly elaborated and specific.

T   F     19. **DIFFERENCE QUESTIONS** are used by Brief Solution-Focused therapists to help clients break out of restrictive beliefs or rules they have about themselves.

T   F     20. **SPARKLING MOMENTS** describe instances in which the client's actions are not dominated by their problems.

# CHAPTER 14 OUTLINE

**CHAPTER FOURTEEN**
**Brief Theories**

I. **BACKGROUND**
    A. Brief Counseling and Psychotherapy
    B. Brief Solution-Focused Therapy
    C. Systematic Treatment Selection for Brief Counseling

II. **HUMAN NATURE**
    A. Brief Solution-Focused Therapy
    B. Systematic Treatment Selection for Brief Counseling

III. **MAJOR CONSTRUCTS**
    A. Brief Solution-Focused Therapy
    B. Systematic Treatment Selection for Brief Counseling

IV. **APPLICATIONS:**
    A. Overview
       1. Brief Solution-Focused Therapy
       2.. Systematic Treatment Selection for Brief Counseling
    B. Goals of Counseling and Psychotherapy
       1. Brief Solution-Focused Therapy
       2. Systematic Treatment Selection for Brief Counseling
    C. The Process of Change
       1. Brief Solution-Focused Therapy
       2. Systematic Treatment Selection for Brief Counseling
    D. Intervention Strategies
       1. Brief Solution-Focused Therapy
       2. Systematic Treatment Selection for Brief Counseling
          a. Client Selection Criteria for Brief Counseling
          b. Selecting Treatments

V. **EVALUATION**
    A. Overview
    B. Supporting Research
    C. Limitations
       1. Brief Solution-Focused Therapy
       2. Systematic Treatment Selection for Brief Counseling

VI. **THE CASE OF MARIA: A BRIEF APPROACH**

VII. **REFERENCES**

**CHAPTER OVERVIEW**

This chapter explores brief counseling and psychotherapy theory through the presentation of two models: Brief Solution-Focused Therapy and Systematic Treatment Selection for brief counseling. This is a small sample of a large and varied literature on brief counseling and psychotherapy. The limitations of over emphasizing treatment length to define brief therapy models are explored as is some of the outcome research on treatment length.

Brief Solution-Focused Therapy grew out of the philosophy of social constructionism. Foundational assumptions include the belief that clients create meaning in social contexts. Thus, there is no objective reality per se that can be separated from the interpretations clients make of life events and experiences.

Systematic Treatment Selection is an eclectic model of therapy based on several theories of psychotherapy. The goal of this model is to provide counselors with decision making criteria for selecting interventions that are best suited for their clients and their problems. Systematic Treatment Selection focuses on outcome research to inform practice. The issue of frequency and duration of treatment is addressed directly for each client based on client resources, problem type and complexity, available therapy interventions, and therapy relationship factors.

BSFT is a mental health resource model that views clients as experts on their own lives with the resources, strengths, and self correcting tendencies to create solutions to their problems. Practitioners are admonished to free themselves of the language of mental deficit that leads to client dependency (Gergen, 1990). Narrative Therapy grew separately from BSFT but holds similar assumptions about client meaning making and solution creation. However, there are differences between the two theories that have led to the development of different interventions.

In BSFT the goals of counseling are changing the viewing and the doing. The process of change is not a rigid one and therefore counselors must maintain flexibility in assisting clients to develop solutions. Questioning strategies and tasks are used by Brief Solution-Focused therapists to promote change. Therapists help clients separate themselves from their problem and through this new relationship with their difficulties clients are assisted in creating solutions. The Brief Solution-Focused therapist's stance toward the client is one of respect and appreciation for the clients resourcefulness.

Systematic Treatment Selection for brief counseling is used with clients having symptom and conflict focused problems. Selection criteria from cognitive behavioral and brief psychodynamic therapy can be used to identify clients appropriate for brief problem or conflict focused counseling. Many factors enable brief counseling including clients with good internal and external resources, circumscribed and acute problems, and therapists able to rapidly assess and establish rapport with clients.

Research on brief counseling and psychotherapy has claimed efficacy for a wide array of client problems. BSFT has provided little empirical research relying mostly on client self report of change. This suggest the need for more systematic outcome research for BSFT. STS is research based and draws heavily on the psychotherapy outcome research literature. Some studies have provided support for its major constructs.

## KEY TERMS

Systematic Treatment Selection
Brief counseling and psychotherapy
Outcome research
Technical Eclecticism
Patient predisposing factors
Environments and circumstances
Relationship variables
Strategies and interventions
Integrative treatment strategy
Response specific personality style
Problem complexity
Interpersonal reactance
Environmental stressors
Life strains
Client selection criteria
Social constructionist philosophy
Narrative
Language of mental deficit
The Mental Research Institute (MRI)
Brief therapy project
Brief Family Therapy Center
Focused solution development
Narrative Therapy
Restorying
Story making
Externalizing the problem
Sparkling moments

Clinical wisdom
Diagnostic systems
Electicism
Meaning making
Construction of reality
Post-modern philosophy
Objective reality
Self-correcting tendencies
Objectification
Collaborative dialogue
Social contexts
Clients as experts
Changing the viewing
Changing the doing
Socializing
Setting the agenda
Exception-oriented questions
Presuppositional questions
Miracle questions
Scaling questions
Difference questions
Formula first session tasks
Observation tasks
Do Something Different Tasks
Personal agency and power
Unique outcomes

## KEY PEOPLE

L. Beutler
S. de Shazer
J. Haley
R. Fisch
M. White
M. Foucault

J. Clarkin
M. Erickson
D. Jackson
I. Insoo Kim Berg
D. Epston

## CLASSROOM EXERCISES TO ENHANCE INSTRUCTION AND STUDENT LEARNING

1. Form groups of 4 to 6 students to serve as treatment planning teams. Provide students with case studies of clients who have different internal and external resources (i.e., ego strength, family support, income, insurance coverage) and have problems of differing seriousness and complexity (i.e., acute vs. chronic). Create different treatment contexts (i.e., community mental health, university counseling, school, private practice) and include limitations based on different settings and funding mechanisms (i.e., agency or school with 10 session treatment limits, private practice with no treatment limits but requiring fee for service, etc.). Teams are to assign treatment and/or recommend referral. Referrals should include specific plans for their disposition.

   After treatment teams have developed a thorough treatment plan ask each to present it to the class. Compare and contrast the ways in which various client, institutional, and economic factors affect treatment plans. Discuss clinical considerations in these varied recommendations as well as any ethical issues they raise.

2. Form groups of 4 to 6 students who are now employed by a major health resource think tank. The federal government has commissioned the think tank to identify those factors most salient to effective and brief mental health treatment. These factors will help form new legislation on mental health coverage which will include the providers who will be able to be reimbursed for services through governmental and private insurance companies. Each think tank team must identify the factors most important to treating clients generally seen in outpatient mental health services whose disorders range from adjustment disorder to depression, anxiety, and posttraumatic stress disorder. Emphasis should be placed on brief therapy. General categories of variables that should be considered include client factors/characteristics, environmental factors, (counseling) relationship factors, and type of intervention.

   Each team should present its findings to the class.

3. Provide a case example to teams of 4 to 6 students who are case consultants to a therapist who has been treating a client unsuccessfully with ongoing therapy that is focused on the client's internalized conflicts rooted in childhood experiences. Ask the case consultants to reconceptualize the case from a Brief Solution-Focused Therapy perspective. The case example used should clearly describe the client in terms of diagnosis, problems, defenses, and internalized conflicts so that application of the Solution-Focused Therapy approach is contrasted to a problem and psychopathology focused approach.

   Each team of case consultants should present their recommendations so the class can compare and contrast various approaches to using Brief Solution Focused Therapy.

4. Provide case examples to teams of 4 to 6 students who must use Cognitive Therapy and Brief Psychodynamic Therapy client selection criteria (see chapter) to determine which clients will be accepted for brief counseling in a community mental health agency. Cases should vary in terms of client problem type/complexity and client resources. Also, students should be challenged to consider alternatives for those clients they deem inappropriate for brief counseling. They can use their knowledge of mental health resources in their community to help in brainstorming referral options.

Ask teams to present their results to the class for compare and contrast purposes.

## INDIVIDUAL EXERCISES TO ENHANCE THE STUDENTS' LEARNING

1. Contact 3 counselors/therapists and ask to interview them about their practice. Ask for their views on brief and long term therapy. Who does it work for, who doesn't respond well? How are they affected by agency, school, or insurance policies related to length of treatment they can offer? What model of brief therapy do they use? How were they trained in brief therapy? Was it sufficient?

2. Go to the library and do a search for books on brief therapy. Identify a model of brief therapy you are interested in. Read a book chapter or journal article on this mode of treatment. Compare and contrast to the theories explored in this chapter.

3. Contact the administrator of a mental health agency or school where counseling services are provided. Ask the administrator for his or her perspective on brief counseling. Why doesn't he or she support the use of brief therapy in his or her setting? What agency policies affect the treatment planning decisions therapists make, including the frequency and duration of counseling? If brief therapy is the exclusive model of the agency, how are clients who need additional treatment handled? Do therapists use client selection criteria in determining who should be accepted for brief counseling? If so, how is it used?

4. Describe your philosophy of life and/or beliefs about human nature, pain, distress, and change that underlie your philosophy of counseling. How do they fit or not fit with the notion of brief counseling and the models discussed in this chapter? Ask yourself whether economics should play any role in determining treatment of mental health issues? Why? Why not?

## QUESTIONS FOR STUDY AND DISCUSSION

1. Define brief and long term therapy. Be as specific as possible. Notice the domains and/or factors that go into your definition. Discuss definitions with the class.

2. Considering your beliefs, values, experiences and academic learning define an approach to brief therapy that would best fit you as a counselor. Consider those brief therapies discussed in the chapter as well as those you are familiar with from other learning experiences.

3. Contrast Brief Solution-Focused Therapy to Systematic Treatment Selection of brief therapy interventions. What are the similarities and differences, strengths and limitations? Which do you feel most comfortable with? Why?

4. Consider a specific problem you are currently coping with. Apply some of the concepts from Brief Solution-Focused Therapy to this problem (i.e., exception-oriented questions, presuppositional questions, miracle questions, scaling questions, difference questions, observation tasks, do something different tasks). Write down all the possible ways of working with your problem from this perspective. To the degree it is appropriate and you are comfortable discuss with the class.

5. Identify two practitioners in your community, one who does mostly brief therapy and another who is committed to long term treatment. Interview these clinicians to learn about their views on practicing brief and long term counseling. Look for values, beliefs, personal experience and other influences such as treatment setting and client population that underlie their philosophy of treatment. Discuss your findings with your class.

## SUGGESTED READINGS

Beutler, L., & Clarkin, J. (1990). *Systematic Treatment Selection: Toward targeted therapeutic intervention*. New York: Brunner/Mazel.

Beutler, L.E., Consoli, A.J., & Williams, R.E. (1995). Integrative and eclectic therapies in practice. In B. Bongar and L.E. Beutler (Eds.) *Comprehensive textbook of psychotherapy: Theory and Practice*. New York: Oxford University Press.

Cooper, J. F. (1995). *A primer of brief psychotherapy*. New York: W. W. Norton.

De Jong, P., & Berg, I. K. (1998). *Interviewing for solutions*. Pacific Grove, CA: Brooks/Cole.

de Shazer, S. (1985). *Keys to solution in brief therapy*. New York: W. W. Norton.

de Shazer, S. (1988). *Clues: Investigating solutions in brief therapy*. New York: W. W. Norton.

de Shazer, S. (1990). What is it about brief therapy that works? In J. K. Zeig & S. G. Gilligan (Eds.), *Brief therapy: Myths, methods, and metaphors* (pp. 90-99). New York: Brunner/Mazel.

Gergen, K. J. (1990). Therapeutic professions and the diffusion of deficit. *Journal of Mind and Behavior, 11*, 353-368.

Koss, M. P., & Shiang, J. (1994). Research on brief psychotherapy. In A. E. Bergin & S. L. Garfield (Eds.), *Handbook of psychotherapy and behavior change* (4th ed., pp. 664-700). New York: John Wiley & Sons.

## SUGGESTED READINGS (con't)

Lambert, M. J. (1992). Implications of outcome research for psychotherapy integration. In J. C. Norcross & M. R. Goldfried (Eds.), *Handbook of psychotherapy integration* (pp. 94-129). New York: Basic Books.

Lambert, M.J. & Cattani-Thompson, K. (1996). Current findings regarding the effectiveness of counseling: Implications for practice. *Journal of Counseling and Development,* 74, 601-608.

Monk, G., Winslade, J., Crocket, K., & Epston, D. (Eds.). (1997). *Narrative therapy in practice: The archaeology of hope.* San Francisco: Jossey-Bass Publishers.

O'Hanlon, W. H. (1990). A grand unified theory for brief therapy: Putting problems in context. In J. K. Zeig & S. G. Gilligan (Eds.). *Brief therapy: Myths, methods, and metaphors (pp. 78-89).* New York: Brunner/Mazel.

Posavac, E.J., Carey, R.G., & Posavac, E.V. (1996). *Program evaluation: Methods and case studies.* Prentice Hall.

Wells, R.S., & Giannetti, V.J. (1990). *Handbook of brief psychotherapies.* New York: Plenum Press.

# CHAPTER POST-INVENTORY

**INSTRUCTIONS: PLEASE ANSWER THE FOLLOWING QUESTIONS NOW THAT YOU HAVE COMPLETED READING THIS CHAPTER.**

T   F      1. Brief Counseling is represented by a small number of **UNIFORM THEORIES**.

T   F      2. **BRIEF AND LONG TERM COUNSELING** are two distinct and clearly delineated approaches to treatment.

T   F      3. **THE AVERAGE NUMBER OF SESSIONS** for clients receiving outpatient counseling is often reported as 6 with a mode of 1 session.

T   F      4. In addition to specific counseling interventions, several domains or "factors" such as the nature of the **THERAPY RELATIONSHIP** and **CLIENT RESOURCES** help predict client change.

T   F      5. **SYSTEMATIC TREATMENT SELECTION** is an attempt to develop an integrated, holistic approach to counselor decision making based on factors found to be most predictive of client change.

T   F      6. According to Systematic Treatment Selection theory, the inability of research to define specific **DECISION MAKING CRITERIA** for selecting appropriate counseling interventions is based on imprecise diagnostic systems and researchers focusing on variables not deemed relevant by clinicians.

T   F      7. **COUNSELING RELATIONSHIP FACTORS** such as credibility, genuineness, and caring are definable and counselors can be trained to make conscious use of them.

T   F      8. Systematic Treatment Selection used for brief counseling interventions focuses on client diagnosis and rarely addresses **ENVIRONMENTAL FACTORS** that may cause distress.

T   F      9. Systematic Treatment Selection does not address **CLIENT SELECTION CRITERIA** for brief counseling.

T   F      10. Systematic Treatment Selection used for brief counseling emphasizes clinical wisdom over **PSYCHOTHERAPY OUTCOME RESEARCH**.

T   F      11. **SOCIAL CONSTRUCTIONIST PHILOSOPHY** contributed to the development of Brief Solution-Focused Therapy.

T   F      12. BSFT focuses on client strengths and may be considered to be a **MENTAL HEALTH RESOURCE MODEL**.

T    F    13. **MILTON ERICKSON** is an important figure in the development of brief psychotherapy.

T    F    14. **NARRATIVE THERAPY** and BSFT share some overlapping concepts concerning the way in which people interpret their experiences.

T    F    15. Clients' inherent **SELF CORRECTING TENDENCIES** are an important part of the change equation for BSFT.

T    F    16. Client diagnosis helps **BRIEF SOLUTION FOCUSED** therapists determine treatment goals.

T    F    17. Brief Solution Focused therapists see themselves as **EXPERTS** on their clients' difficulties and solutions.

T    F    18. In BSFT **CLIENT SELECTION CRITERIA** are clearly elaborated and specific.

T    F    19. **DIFFERENCE QUESTIONS** are used by Brief Solution-Focused therapists to help clients break out of restrictive beliefs or rules they have about themselves.

T    F    20. **SPARKLING MOMENTS** describe instances in which the client's actions are not dominated by their problems.

# NOTES

158

# CHAPTER FIFTEEN
## *EASTERN THEORIES*

**CHAPTER PRE-INVENTORY**

**INSTRUCTIONS: PLEASE ANSWER THE FOLLOWING QUESTIONS BEFORE YOU READ THIS CHAPTER.**

T    F    1. A focus on **CALM AND CONTEMPLATION** in everyday life is a basic concept of Eastern philosophy.

T    F    2. In the Eastern tradition, an **OBLIGATION TO FAMILY** is paramount.

T    F    3. **MORITA THERAPY** is both an Asian and Eurocentric approach to psycho-therapy.

T    F    4. The construct of **NATURALISM** relates to an acceptance of the world as it is.

T    F    5. In Morita therapy, **NEUROSIS IS VIEWED AS PATHOLOGICAL.**

T    F    6. In Morita therapy, the therapist gives the client **PERMISSION TO FEEL OR THINK** whatever he/she is feeling or thinking.

T    F    7. In Japan, **HOMOPHOBIA** indicates a fear or dislike of homosexuals.

T    F    8. The Japanese philosophy toward **ATTENTION** is directed toward the inner self, not society as a whole.

T    F    9. Clients of Morita therapy may typically have prescribed for them a week of **COMPLETE BED REST.**

T    F    10. In Morita therapy, one technique used to assist the client is acknowledging experiences **MOMENT-BY-MOMENT IN THE LEARNING OF WORK.**

T    F    11. A client in Morita therapy is considered to be **CURED** when he/she feels happier and understands what must be done to maintain the happiness.

T    F    12. Morita is closely associated with the **PHENOMENOLOGICAL** approach to counseling.

T    F    13. The **SHINKEISHITSU** condition is Morita therapy suggests that the client is filled with worries and excessive anxieties.

**T F** 14. A necessary condition for successful Morita therapy is a **POSITIVE CLIENT-COUNSELOR RELATIONSHIP.**

**T F** 15. **EXPERIENTIAL LEARNING** is critical to the practice of Morita therapy.

**T F** 16. Three basic concepts of Morita therapy are **WORK, PHYSICAL ACTIVITY, AND ACTING/DOING.**

**T F** 17. In the **DIARY** work of the client, he/she is given an outline of what specifically is to be written day-to-day to help with focus.

**T F** 18. Inpatient and outpatient Morita therapy uses **BIBLIOTHERAPY** as a strategy for counseling.

**T F** 19. Current research on the efficacy of using Morita therapy indicates that it is appropriate for a **DIVERSE, MULTICULTURAL POPULATION BASE.**

**T F** 20. The concept that indicates that an individual has accepted life's outcomes "as they are" is **ARUGAMAMA.**

# CHAPTER 15 OUTLINE

**CHAPTER FIFTEEN**
**Eastern Theories**

## I. INTRODUCTION
    A. Eastern Psychological Thought
    B. Eastern Mental Health Practice
    C. An Introduction to Morita Therapy

## II. BACKGROUND

## III. HUMAN NATURE
    A. Family and <u>Amae</u>
    B. Collectivism
    C. Naturalism

## IV. MAJOR CONSTRUCTS
    A. Neurosis
    B. <u>Shinkeishitsu</u>
    C. Misfocused mind
    D. Control
    E. Homophobia
    F. <u>Arugamama</u>
    G. Meaningful Life
    H. Work
    I. Cure

## V. APPLICATIONS
    A. Overview
    B. Goals of Counseling and Psychotherapy
    C. The Process of Change
        1. Pre-Therapy Phase
        2. Phase 1: Absolute, Isolated Bed Rest
        3. Phase 2: Light Work Therapy
        4. Phase 3: Heavier Mental and Physical Work Therapy
        5. Phase 4: Life Activities Training Therapy
    D. Intervention Strategies
        1. Bed Rest
        2. Personal Counseling: Guidance and Instruction
        3. Work
        4. Diary
        5. Meditation
        6. Readings
        7. Homework and Guided Activities

## CHAPTER OVERVIEW

This chapter offers an overview of the basic philosophies of Eastern psychological thought and mental health practice, with Morita therapy as a specific approach developed in detail. Included in the overview of traditional Eastern thought are concepts essential to understanding the mental health perspective of Eastern cultures. These concepts include: purification, "agape" or unconditional love" and "ki" which represents psychological energy.

Morita therapy emphasizes a basic view of human nature as optimistic, natural, and for the most part, decent. Morita is a natural phenomena that cannot be controlled. A meaningful life can be achieved only through acceptance of the life environment as it is.

There are four phases that occur during the counseling process. The chapter includes an explanation of each phase, with description of each specific phase. Intervention strategies are discussed, as well as goals for the therapy. The chapter concludes with the evaluation of Morita therapy, incorporating the supporting research and also detailing the limitations of the process. Some limitations are that Morita therapy may not be appropriate for specific populations, such as women in general and mid-life or older adults; research is available only on specific, narrowly defined populations, that do not include individuals presenting with specific disorders or pathology.

## KEY TERMS

Morita therapy
Eastern psychotherapy
Ethical thought
Ethical conduct
Mental force
Purification
Buddhism
Cultural lens
**Arugamama**
Naturalism
Family unit
Bed rest
**On**
**Wa**
Acceptance
Meaningful life
Cure
**Tatemae**
Neurasthenia
Obsessional fears
Accomplishment

Contemplation
Meditation
Yoga
Individual will
**KI**
**Agape**
Eurocentric
Western perspective
Experiential
**Shinkeishitsu**
Social obligation
**Amae**
Collectivism
Sense of self
**Toraware**
**Homophobia**
Neurosis
Egocentricity
Anxiety neurosis
Light work therapy
Phenomenological

## KEY TERMS (con't)

Outer world

Misfocused mind

Fumon

**Ma**

Diary

Bibliotherapy

Refocusing

Regime

Negativity

Unselfishness

Personal well-being

Constructive living instruction

Existentialism

Person-centered therapy

Existing realities

**Sei no yokubo**

Discovery of live organization

**Jibun**

Self-absorbed

**Kowa**

Attention shift

**Work**

Behavioral purpose

Morita Lifeway

Doing/behavior

Ideal psychological health

Generosity

Mind-body focus

Peace

**Honne**

Cognitive-behavioral therapy

Psychoanalytic therapy

Family-like environment

**Tanin**

**Miuichi**

**Giri**


## KEY PEOPLE

S. Morita

R. Walsh

P. Bankart

K. Ohara

K. Kitanishi

F. Ishigama

R. Suzuki

A. Kondo

D. Reynolds

D. Takeo

T. Kora

L. James Hedstrom

A. Mori

T. Suzuki

C. Fujita


## CLASSROOM EXERCISES TO ENHANCE INSTRUCTION AND STUDENT LEARNING

1. Divide the class into groups of 4-5 asking each group to select ten words/terms mentioned in the chapter that seem unfamiliar. Each group will then list the terms and, from the explanation in the chapter, define the words/terms in his/her own words to assist with proper meaning. Each group will have a spokesperson chosen by the group members, who will report two to four of the terms to the class, so that most of the new words/terms in the chapter become clear through discussion.

2. Request that the class participate in a "meditation journey" with you as facilitator. Choose an exercise for beginning meditation, such as slowly counting ten breaths, in an out, with no interruption of mental focus. Explain to the students that if they are disconnected before reaching the 10th breath, they will begin counting again from one. Ask them to close their eyes, clear the desk, and place both feet flat on the floor, and if possible, face the sun. Conduct a total group discussion at the end of this exercise, emphasizing the sense of calm and contemplation that is possible to achieve through Eastern meditative training.

3. Divide the class into three groups, giving each group a brief description of a client presenting with **Shinkeishitsu** symptoms. Ask each group to develop a role-play simulation for that client using the Morita therapy approach. Each group will develop the character of the client and the counselor, and be able to role-play the scenario in a fishbowl for the class. Conduct a total group discussion on the three versions of the scenario.

4. Assign the class a short research paper (8-12 pages) on one of the following topics; traditional Eastern religious/philosophical thought; current practice in Eastern mental health, excluding Morita therapy; or a comparison of Eastern and Western cultures in current mental health practice. Each student will present a 5-minute synopsis of the paper to the entire class before handing it in.

## INDIVIDUAL EXERCISES TO ENHANCE THE STUDENTS' LEARNING

1. Conduct a personal survey of your level of **arugamama** (acceptance of reality as it is).
   a. Record in writing the "upsets" you experience every day for a week.
   b. Read each entry the day after you write it; reframe that particular "upset" to reflect acceptance of what is.
   c. Your last entry for the week should include a list of reframed "upsets" and how, using the Morita approach, you have restated them.

2. Begin to keep a diary as indicated for use in Morita therapy. As you review the information in the chapter about the use of the diary as an intervention, begin writing your thoughts and feelings, and what you feel your **work** (accomplishment) has been on a daily basis. Write each day for two weeks, about one page a day. At the end of the writing, summarize your experiences and share with the entire class.

3. Based upon your specific area of interest, i.e, eating disorders, aging, gender diversity, career and lifestyle issues, investigate how the Morita approach might be used in counseling that population. Use library research, personal interviews, obtain timely non-scholarly periodicals such as Quest, for example, to read about current thinking. Share what you find with the class.

4. Investigate the availability of meditation or yoga training in the area. Ask to observe or take part in a training session; interview the instructor on his/her philosophy of Eastern tradition and culture.

5. Design a scenario, using Morita therapy, for a client of your choice and imagination. Develop a treatment plan, including presenting issue, diagnosis, long and short term goals, and interventions. Write the plan according to how you think a Morita therapist would translate the Western concepts into an Eastern psychotherapeutic model. Share with the entire class.

## QUESTIONS FOR STUDY AND DISCUSSION

1. As you review the five basic goals of Morita therapy, which are: focus the mind away from the self; accept self and world **arugamama;** social/moral responsibility; live constructive lives; and recognition of purpose, how do they differ from some of the Western therapeutic approaches, i.e. Person-centered or Cognitive-behavioral?

2. What position do you take on the following question? "A Morita therapist would not be concerned with cause. Neither the etiology nor causes are explored with clients. Such introspection only causes clients to turn further inward, obsess more on themselves, rather than focus on the outer world and what needs to be done."

3. What benefit is derived from the traditional prescription of "complete bed rest" for the **Shinkeishitsu** client? Is it possible for the essence of that particular technique to be used in selected forms of Western therapy? How might that happen?

4. As you read the chapter, the intervention strategies emphasize the experiential component. Imagine an experiential intervention strategy NOT mentioned, and then imagine how that could be used with the Morita client

## SUGGESTED READINGS

Claxton, G. (1986). (Ed.). *Beyond therapy: The impact of Eastern religions on psychological theory and practice.* London: Wisdom Press.

Goldberger, N .R. (1996). Cultural imperatives and diversity in ways of knowing. In N. Goldberger, J. Tarule, B. Clinchy, & M. Belenky (Eds). *Knowledge, difference and power.* New York: Basic Books.

Hoover, T. (1977). *Zen culture.* New York: Random.

Hsu, F.L.K. (1985). The self in cross-cultural perspective. In A. Marsella, G. DeVos & F.L.K. Hsu (Eds.). *Culture and the self.* London: Tavistock.

Kabat-Zinn, J. (1993). *Where ever you go, there you are.* New York: Hyperion.

Walsh, R. & Vaughan, F. (Eds.). (1993). *Paths beyond ego: The transpersonal vision.* Los Angeles: J.P. Tarcher.

**CHAPTER POST-INVENTORY**

**INSTRUCTIONS: PLEASE ANSWER THE FOLLOWING QUESTIONS NOW THAT YOU HAVE COMPLETED READING THIS CHAPTER.**

T   F      1. A focus on **CALM AND CONTEMPLATION** in everyday life is a basic concept of Eastern philosophy.

T   F      2. In the Eastern tradition, an **OBLIGATION TO FAMILY** is paramount.

T   F      3. **MORITA THERAPY** is both an Asian and Eurocentric approach to psycho-therapy.

T   F      4. The construct of **NATURALISM** relates to an acceptance of the world as it is.

T   F      5. In Morita therapy, **NEUROSIS** IS VIEWED AS PATHOLOGICAL.

T   F      6. In Morita therapy, the therapist gives the client **PERMISSION TO FEEL OR THINK** whatever he/she is feeling or thinking.

T   F      7. IN JAPAN, **HOMOPHOBIA** indicates a fear or dislike of homosexuals.

T   F      8. The Japanese philosophy toward **ATTENTION** is directed toward the inner self, not society as a whole.

T   F      9. Clients of Morita therapy may typically have prescribed for them a week of **COMPLETE BED REST.**

T   F     10. In Morita therapy, one technique used to assist the client is acknowledging experiences **MOMENT-BY-MOMENT IN THE LEARNING OF WORK.**

T   F     11. A client in Morita therapy is considered to be **CURED** when he/she feels happier and understands what must be done to maintain the happiness.

T   F     12. Morita is closely associated with the **PHENOMENOLOGICAL** approach to counseling.

T   F     13. The **SHINKEISHITSU** condition is Morita therapy suggests that the client is filled with worries and excessive anxieties.

T   F     14. A necessary condition for successful Morita therapy is a **POSITIVE CLIENT-COUNSELOR RELATIONSHIP.**

T   F     15. **EXPERIENTIAL LEARNING** is critical to the practice of Morita therapy.

T　F　16. Three basic concepts of Morita therapy are **WORK, PHYSICAL ACTIVITY, AND ACTING/DOING.**

T　F　17. In the **DIARY** work of the client, he/she is given an outline of what specifically is to be written day-to-day to help with focus.

T　F　18. Inpatient and outpatient Morita therapy uses **BIBLIOTHERAPY** as a strategy for counseling.

T　F　19. Current research on the efficacy of using Morita therapy indicates that it is appropriate for a **DIVERSE, MULTICULTURAL POPULATION BASE.**

T　F　20. The concept that indicates that an individual has accepted life's outcomes "as they are" is **ARUGAMAMA.**

# CHAPTER SIXTEEN
## *Counseling and Psychotherapy with Children*

**CHAPTER PRE-INVENTORY**

**INSTRUCTIONS: PLEASE ANSWER THE FOLLOWING QUESTIONS BEFORE YOU READ THIS CHAPTER.**

T    F     1. **PHYSIOLOGICAL CHANGES** in the brain are minimal after birth.

T    F     2. **ENCULTURATION** is the process of adapting to the dominant culture.

T    F     3. Bruner's **SYMBOLIC STAGE** is roughly equivalent to Piaget's formal operations period.

T    F     4. The **WHORF-SAPIR HYPOTHESIS** states that thought shapes language.

T    F     5. According to Maslow, children's need for love and need for belongingness precedes their **NEED FOR SAFETY.**

T    F     6. Since the 1989 UN Convention on the Rights of the Child treaty, 11 to 17 year old **CHILDREN'S RIGHTS** in the United States have been expanded and include the legal right to consent to treatment.

T    F     7. The ability to give **INFORMED CONSENT** is based on three standards: knowing, voluntary, and competence.

T    F     8. The child's **RIGHT TO PRIVACY** is not guaranteed legally.

T    F     9. **CONFIDENTIALITY** is a problematic concept for counselors working with children because one must decide whether the child or the parent is the client.

T    F     10. The **DUTY TO REPORT** suspected child abuse and neglect is a legal requirement only for psychologists who are licensed.

T    F     11. The **PSYCHODYNAMIC MODEL** frequently is applied to counseling children in schools.

T    F     12. The **BEHAVIORAL MODEL** is based on the belief that psychopathology results from imposed social and environmental conditions that interfere with personal growth.

**T  F** 13. Counseling using the **CLIENT-CENTERED MODEL** requires empathic understanding, unconditional positive regard, and general acceptance of the child as a person.

**T  F** 14. The **FAMILY MODEL** of counseling assumes that pathology lies in the interactions between family members.

**T  F** 15. The **INTEGRATED INTERPERSONAL MODEL** for individual school-based counseling utilizes an integration of theoretical approaches and involves interventions with systems impacting the child.

**T  F** 16. Common recurring stages in children's **SAND PLAY** include chaos, struggle, and resolution.

**T  F** 17. **WATER PLAY** is a useful therapeutic technique for children who are aggressive or need to relax.

**T  F** 18. To use **MUSIC THERAPY** the counselor must be musically talented.

**T  F** 19. **BIBLIOTHERAPY** is not used widely by elementary school counselors because it often interferes with the reading program in schools.

**T  F** 20. Children's **STORYTELLING** rarely parallels the events of their lives.

# CHAPTER 16 OUTLINE

**CHAPTER SIXTEEN**
**Counseling and Psychotherapy With Children**

I. **THE CHILD IN TODAY'S WORLD**
   A. Safety
   B. Redefinitions of Family
   C. Peer Influence
   D. Changing Gender Roles

II. **DEVELOPMENTAL PERSPECTIVES**
   A. Physical Growth
   B. Cultural Learning
   C. Cognitive Growth
   D. Language Growth
   E. Social and Behavioral Growth
   F. Emotional and Personality Growth

III. **LEGAL AND ETHICAL ISSUES**
   A. Informed Consent
   B. Privacy
   C. Confidentiality
   D. Duty to Warn and to Report Child Abuse

IV. **TREATMENT SETTING ISSUES**
   A. The Environment
   B. The Referral Process
   C. Goals of Counseling
   D. Confidentiality in Schools
   E. Termination of Counseling

V. **CHILD TREATMENT ISSUES**

VI. **MODELS FOR COUNSELING CHILDREN**
   A. The Medical Model
   B. The Psychodynamic Model
   C. The Behavioral Model
   D. The Client-Centered Model
   E. The Family Model
   F. An Integrated, Interpersonal Model for Counseling in Schools

VII. **COUNSELING TECHNIQUES FOR OLDER CHILDREN**

**VIII. COUNSELING TECHNIQUES FOR YOUNGER CHILDREN**
   A. Play as a Medium
      1. Toys as Tools
      2. Sand and Water Play
   B. Therapeutic activities
      1. Art
      2. Music
      3. Bibliotherapy
      4. Storytelling
      5. Other techniques

**IX.   SUMMARY**

**X.    REFERENCES**

## CHAPTER OVERVIEW

In an effort to provide background information as a basis for counselors to understand the conditions that children of today face, this chapter provides an overview of changing conditions for children during the last half of the twentieth century, including conditions related to safety, redefinitions of the family, peer influences, and gender roles. Developmental issues also impact children's abilities to communicate adequately and to understand other's communications. A discussion of physical growth and cultural learning, with theories about development in the areas of cognitive, language, social, behavioral, emotional, and personality growth, are provided to give the counselor a foundation for judging the child's abilities based on age and other personal characteristics. Additionally, legal and ethical issues related to counseling children are discussed, with special emphasis on issues of informed consent, privacy, confidentiality, duty to warn, and duty to report child abuse.

Because counseling children occurs primarily in two settings (i.e., school and clinic), differences in these environments, referral processes, goals of counseling, keeping confidences, and termination of counseling are discussed. Other issues which differentiate child counseling from adult counseling are discussed as well. Six models for counseling children also are presented: medical, psychodynamic, behavioral, client-centered, family, and integrated models. Finally, counseling techniques for older children are discussed briefly. Techniques for younger children that are presented include play therapy, with a discussion of toys as tools as well as sand and water play, and therapeutic activities such as art therapy, music therapy, bibliotherapy, storytelling, computer games, and physical activities. Other sources for therapeutic techniques for children are provided for the reader.

## KEY TERMS

Absolute confidentiality
Acculturation
Autonomy vs. shame and doubt
Belongingness and love needs
Blended families
Client-centered model
Concrete operations period
Cultural norms
Ego identity vs. role confusion
Enactive stage
Equilibration
Ethnic identity
Formal operations period
Gender identity
Generativity vs. self-absorption
Iconic stage
Information-processing
Initiative vs. guilt

Accommodation
Art therapy
Behavioral model
Bibliotherapy
Children's rights
Competent consent
Confidentiality
Child abuse duty to warn
Ego integrity vs. despair
Enculturation
Esteem needs
Family model
Foster care
Gender roles
Homelessness
Industry vs. inferiority
Informed consent
Intimacy vs. isolation

## KEY TERMS (con't)

Integrated interpersonal model
Knowing consent
Latch key children
Medical model
Nuclear families
Physiological changes
Play therapy
Prevention
Psychosocial stage development theory
Right to privacy
Sand play
Self-identity
Sexual exploitation
Socialization patterns
Storytelling
Trust vs. mistrust
Voluntary consent
Water play

Involuntary submission
Language acquisition device
Limited confidentiality
Music therapy
Peer influence
Physiological needs
Preoperational period
Psychodynamic model
Racial identity
Safety needs
Self-actualization
Sensorimotor period
Single parent families
Step families
Symbolic stage
Universal grammar
Vygotsky's hypothesis
Whorf-Sapir hypothesis

## KEY PEOPLE

V. Axline
M. Bowen
N. Chomsky
A. Freud
H. Hug-Hellmuth
A. Maslow
J. Piaget
E. Sapir
L. Vygotsky

A. Bandura
J. Bruner
E. Erikson
S. Freud
M. Klein
I. Pavlov
C. Rogers
B. Skinner
B. Whorf

## CLASSROOM EXERCISES TO ENHANCE INSTRUCTION AND STUDENT LEARNING

1. Divide the class into groups of three or four students each and have each group elect a reporter. Provide each group with a one page bulleted summary of a child's background and problems the child is having in school. After having read the summary, the group should brainstorm what approach they would take next to help the child and what further information they will need to get from parents, teachers, and the child in order to better understand how to help the child. After five minutes of brainstorming, bring the groups together and have the reporters list what their group found.

2. Divide the class into two groups, designating one as "parent advocates" and the other as "child advocates," to debate the proposal to ratify the 1989 UN Convention on the Rights of the Child treaty in the United States. What are the benefits for the child and when do children's rights interfere with parents' rights?

3. Divide the class into dyads. Each dyad should designate one person as the "teacher" and the other as the "counselor." Each dyad should role play the counselor giving feedback about counseling progress to the child's teacher, with the teacher probing for more information. The counselor should exhibit skills in diplomacy, respect for the teacher, and protecting the child's confidentiality, while giving the teacher enough information to work effectively with the child. After five minutes, the dyad members should change positions, giving both members time to practice these skills.

## INDIVIDUAL EXERCISES TO ENHANCE THE STUDENTS' LEARNING

1. Each student should choose a therapeutic technique for working with children that is of special interest to the student. Gather information on the technique and then present it to the class, discussing how the technique is implemented, identifying special considerations to keep in mind when using the technique, and modeling the technique.

2. Write a research paper on the efficacy of using a particular theoretical orientation in counseling children with a particular disorder. The choice of orientation and disorder should follow the student's special interests.

3. Identify a child in your neighborhood whose parents will give permission for you to spend an hour talking and playing with him or her. Using play materials and skills necessary for developing a relationship with a child, interact with the child in ways you would if you were conducting the first counseling session with the child. Be sure to talk to the child about confidentiality and its limits. Report to the class what age the child is, what happened and what you learned when working with this child.

## QUESTIONS FOR STUDY AND DISCUSSION

1. Discuss the present conditions and experiences of children who live in inner city areas. In rural areas. In suburbs. In small towns. How are these conditions and experiences similar and different from those experienced by children thirty years ago? How do the differences impact children's lives?

2. Discuss the effects of cultural learning on cognitive, language, social, behavioral, emotional, and personality growth. How might cultural learning be similar and different for children who live in a neighborhood made up of members of their cultural group, compared to those who live among members of many different

cultural groups?  How might socioeconomic status impact one's cultural learning?

3. Discuss the effects on the legal system of the ratification of the 1989 UN Convention on the Rights of the Child by the U.S. Government.  What impact would the ratification have on legal and ethical practice for counselors?

4. Discuss the school environment and its potential effect on the practice of counseling children in schools.  How might the counselor structure the counseling program in schools to minimize the negative effects of the system on counseling children and enhance the understanding and cooperation of school personnel in building an emotionally healthy school environment?

5. Discuss ways the counselor can minimize the negative effects of children's limited understanding of counseling and enhance their participation and cooperation in the counseling process.

6. Discuss children's vulnerability and identify advice that, as a counselor, you would not want to give children.  Brainstorm potential messages that are inappropriate for children and those that are appropriate.

## SUGGESTED READINGS

Brown, D.T. & Prout, H.T. (Eds.). (1989).  *Counseling and psychotherapy with children and adolescents: Theory and practice for school and clinical settings* (2nd. Ed.). Brandon, VT: Clinical Psychology Publishing Co.

Bruner, J. (1986). Play, thought and language. *Prospects*, XVI, 77-83.

D'Amato, R.C., & Rothlisberg, B.A. (Eds.). (1992). *Psychological perspectives on interventions: A case approach to prescriptions for change*. NY: Longman.

Ehly, S. & Dustin, R. (1989). *Individual and group counseling in schools*. NY: Guilford Press.

Garbarino, J., Stott, F.M., & Faculty of the Erikson Institute. (1989). *What children can tell us*. San Francisco, CA: Jossey-Bass Publishers.

Hayworth, M. (1964). *Child psychotherapy: Theory and practice*. NY: Basic Books.

James, B. (1989). *Treating traumatized children: New insights and creative interventions*. Lexington, Massachusetts: Lexington Books.

Kendall, P.C. (1991). *Child and adolescent therapy*. NY: Guilford Press.

Landreth, G.L. (1996).  *Play therapy interventions with children's problems*. Northvale, NJ: Jason Aronson.

Kratochwill, T.R. & Morris, R.J. (Eds.). (1991).  *The practice of child therapy* (2nd ed.). New York: Pergamon Press.

Kratochwill, T.R. & Morris, R.J. (Eds.). (1993).  *Handbook of psychotherapy with children and adolescents*.  Boston, MA: Allyn & Bacon.

Pitcher, G.D., & Poland, S. (1992). *Crisis intervention in the schools*. NY: Guilford Press.

## SUGGESTED READINGS (con't)

Poland, S. (1989). *Suicide prevention in the schools*. NY: Guilford Press.

Pope, A.W., McHale, S.M., & Craighead, W.E. (1988). *Self-esteem enhancement with children and adolescents*. New York: Pergamon Press.

Rose, S.D., & Edleson, J.L. (1987). *Working with children and adolescents in groups*. San Francisco, CA: Jossey-Bass.

Sandoval, J. (Ed.). (1988). *Crisis counseling, intervention, and prevention in the schools*. Hillsdale, NJ: Erlbaum.

Stark, K.D. (1990). *Childhood depression: School-based* intervention. NY: Guilford Press.

Vernon, A. (1993). *Counseling children and adolescents*. Denver, CO: Love Publishing Co.

# CHAPTER POST-INVENTORY

**INSTRUCTIONS: PLEASE ANSWER THE FOLLOWING QUESTIONS NOW THAT YOU HAVE COMPLETED READING THIS CHAPTER.**

T  F  1. **PHYSIOLOGICAL CHANGES** in the brain are minimal after birth.

T  F  2. **ENCULTURATION** is the process of adapting to the dominant culture.

T  F  3. Bruner's **SYMBOLIC STAGE** is roughly equivalent to Piaget's formal operations period.

T  F  4. The **WHORF-SAPIR HYPOTHESIS** states that thought shapes language.

T  F  5. According to Maslow, children's need for love and need for belongingness precedes their **NEED FOR SAFETY.**

T  F  6. Since the 1989 UN Convention on the Rights of the Child treaty, 11 to 17 year old **CHILDREN'S RIGHTS** in the United States have been expanded and include the legal right to consent to treatment.

T  F  7. The ability to give **INFORMED CONSENT** is based on three standards: knowing, voluntary, and competence.

T  F  8. The child's **RIGHT TO PRIVACY** is not guaranteed legally.

T  F  9. **CONFIDENTIALITY** is a problematic concept for counselors working with children because one must decide whether the child or the parent is the client.

T  F  10. The **DUTY TO REPORT** suspected child abuse and neglect is a legal requirement only for psychologists who are licensed.

T  F  11. The **PSYCHODYNAMIC MODEL** frequently is applied to counseling children in schools.

T  F  12. The **BEHAVIORAL MODEL** is based on the belief that psychopathology results from imposed social and environmental conditions that interfere with personal growth.

T  F  13. Counseling using the **CLIENT-CENTERED MODEL** requires empathic understanding, unconditional positive regard, and general acceptance of the child as a person.

T  F  14. The **FAMILY MODEL** of counseling assumes that pathology lies in the interactions between family members.

T  F   15. The **INTEGRATED INTERPERSONAL MODEL** for individual school-based counseling utilizes an integration of theoretical approaches and involves interventions with systems impacting the child.

T  F   16. Common recurring stages in children's **SAND PLAY** include chaos, struggle, and resolution.

T  F   17. **WATER PLAY** is a useful therapeutic technique for children who are aggressive or need to relax.

T  F   18. To use **MUSIC THERAPY** the counselor must be musically talented.

T  F   19. **BIBLIOTHERAPY** is not used widely by elementary school counselors because it often interferes with the reading program in schools.

T  F   20. Children's **STORYTELLING** rarely parallels the events of their lives.

# NOTES

# CHAPTER SEVENTEEN
## *COUNSELING AND PSYCHOTHERAPY: MULTICULTURAL CONSIDERATIONS*

**CHAPTER PRE-INVENTORY**

**INSTRUCTIONS: PLEASE ANSWER THE FOLLOWING QUESTIONS BEFORE YOU READ THIS CHAPTER:**

T (F) 1. The existence of **CULTURAL BIAS** in counseling and therapy has been documented by many authors. *few*

(T) F 2. The history and legitimacy of **MULTICULTURAL COUNSELING** have paralleled the sociopolitical movements in the United States. *This True*

(T) F 3. Counseling and therapeutic theories address the concept of mental health from the assumption of a universal **(EDIC)** Euro-American point of view, to the exclusion of a cultural-specific **(EMIC)** view.

T (F) 4. **MINORITY** is defined as: A group of people who, because of their physical or cultural characteristics, receive differential and unequal treatment due to collective discrimination.

(T) F ? 5. **WHITE CULTURE** is defined as the synthesis of ideas, values, and beliefs coalesced from descendants of white European ethnic groups in the United States. *Why the US?*

T (F) 6. **ASIAN AMERICANS/PACIFIC ISLANDERS** represent the smallest minority group in the United States

(T) F ? 7. The importance of family is a major consideration for most **MINORITY GROUPS.**

T (F) 8. **STEREOTYPE** is defined as a flexible preconception about members of a particular group without regard for individual variation.

T (F) 9. **HISPANICS** constitute the nation's largest racial and ethnic minority group.

(T) F 10. **ETHNIC GROUPS** from different geographical locations exhibit distinct geocultural traditions and customs.

**T** F     11. **RATIONAL-EMOTIVE AND COGNITIVE-BEHAVIORAL THEORIES** challenge dependency, which to certain minority groups may be counterproductive to their concept of interdependency, an important part of their cultural values and one they view as essentially healthy.

**T** F     12. **EXISTENTIAL THEORY** is based on the understanding of the individual and allows the freedom to use other systems and techniques that can be made applicable to racial and ethnic groups.

T **F**     13. By the year 2010, **WHITES** will represent 90% of the total population.

T **F**     14. The term **NATIVE AMERICAN** is limited to only American Indians.

**T** F     15. **ACCULTURATION** is composed of numerous dimensions, such as cultural values, ideologies, ethnic identity, beliefs, attitudes toward self, majority language use, cultural customs, practices, and ethnic perceptions.

**T** F     16. **HISPANICS** comprise a large diverse group composed of Mexican Americans, Puerto Ricans, Cuban Americans, South and Central Americans, and others.

T **F**     17 **AFRICAN AMERICANS** constitute the nation's second largest racial and ethnic minority group.

See 9

**T** F     18. When working with **MINORITY CLIENTS** who still use their language of origin, understanding the language is not enough for the counseling/therapeutic practitioner.

T **F**     19. For the minority groups presented in this chapter, the concept of **TIME** is very similar to the majority view in which the focus is the future; you sacrifice for tomorrow, and postpone gratification.

**T** F     20. Counselors or therapists must be aware of the self-referent labels that clients choose. This is especially true for **MINORITY CLIENTS**.

# CHAPTER 17 OUTLINE

**CHAPTER SEVENTEEN**
**Counseling and Psychotherapy: Multicultural Considerations**

I.   **NATIVE AMERICANS, AFRICAN AMERICANS, HISPANIC AMERICANS, AND ASIAN AMERICANS/PACIFIC ISLANDERS**

II.   **DEFINITIONS**

III.   **COUNSELOR AND THERAPIST SELF-AWARENESS**

IV.   **ACCULTURATION**

V.   **DEMOGRAPHICS**
   A. Native Americans
   B. African Americans
   C. Hispanic Americans
   D. Asian Americans/Pacific Islanders

VI.   **RACIAL AND ETHNIC CULTURAL CONSIDERATIONS**
   A. Language  *— Affective meaning*
   B. Cultural Identity  *— Self Referent Labels / ID stage Dev.*
   C. Generation  *⇒ for Acculturation*
   D. Cultural Custom Styles  *< Respect Eldest — Obedience / Patience/Respect — Eye Contact*
   E. Geographical Location and Neighborhoods  *— Ethnic Area / Integrated N'hood / only minority*
   F. Family Constituency  *— definitions of family*
   G. Psychohistorical and Religious Traditions  *— Child Rearing – Cooperative r.t competitive*
   H. Individuality  *or tribe / or / family  — Pastors etc*

VII.   **RACIAL AND ETHNIC CULTURAL COMPONENTS**  *for Theories*
   A. Language
   ◯ B. Family and Social Relations
   ✳ C. Time Focus  *Big One*
   ✳ D. Nature-People Relationships
   E. Holistic View
   ◯ ✳ F. Human Activity and Cooperation
   G. Identity
   H. Mental Health
   ◯ I. Spirituality and Religion
   ◯ J. Responsibility
   K. Oppression and Racism

✳ *Being / Becoming*
◯ *Individual / Community*

## VIII. SUMMARY AND CRITIQUE OF THEORIES
  A. Freudian Psychoanalytic Theory
  B. Jungian Analytical Psychology
  C. Adlerian Individual Psychology
  D. Existential Theory
  E. Person-Centered Theory
  F. Gestalt Theory
  G. Cognitive-Behavioral Theories
  I. Reality Therapy Theory
  J. Family Theory
  K. Special Note

## IX. SUMMARY

## X. REFERENCES

## CHAPTER OVERVIEW

In this chapter, current multicultural issues facing our profession are identified, in particular the racial/ethnic considerations impinging upon the current counseling/therapeutic theories. The complexity of multiculturalism in theory has many facets that must be considered; such as demographics, definitions, racial/ethnic/cultural considerations, acculturation, and socioeconomic and cultural distinctions. These considerations do not provide a prescriptive analysis for integration into existing theories but were included because of their importance to the following four focus groups: (1) Native Americans; (2) Hispanic Americans; (3) African Americans; and (4) Asian/Pacific Islanders.

Current counseling/therapeutic theories reflect the "Zeitgeist" of the era and region in which the theorist lived. Therefore, traditional counseling and psychotherapies were developed for white middle and upper-middle class clients. These theories were developed by white practitioners enmeshed in western cultural values and the applicability of these theories is questionable.

With these caveats in mind, the chapter's authors address the following issues as they relate to the four identified focus groups: (1) definitions; (2) overview of multiculturalism; (3) therapist self-awareness; and (4) Euro-American mainstream assumptions.

In addition, a discussion of counseling/therapeutic theories and their appropriateness or adaptability to traditional minority groups is presented in the Counseling Theories Racial/Ethnic Component Chart (17.1), followed by a discussion of each theoretical system's incorporation of multicultural issues. The chapter ends with a summary.

## KEY TERMS

Multicultural
Culturally encapsulated counselor
Multiculturalism
Euro-American individualistic psychology
White values and beliefs
Native American
Asian/Pacific Islander
Ethnicity
Multicultural counseling/psychotherapy
White culture
Cultural integration
Acculturation
Assimilation
Eskimos
Mexican Americans
Cuban Americans

Cultural bias
Cross-cultural awareness
Fourth force
Ethnic minority
African American
Hispanic American
Race
Minority
Stereotypes
Paradigmatic shift
Culturally pluralistic model
Ethnic identity
Diversity
Aleuts
Puerto Ricans
Japanese

## KEY TERMS (con't)

Chinese
Filipinos
Guamans
Samoans
Heterogenous groups
Language
Generation
Psychological and religious traditions
Cultural mental health
Melting pot philosophy
Psychoanalytic
Social interest
Chicano
American of Mexican decent
Neighborhoods
Specific racial/ethnic cultural components
Time focus
Holistic view
Emic
Spirituality
Adlerian/systems theory
Analytic Psychology
Gestalt
Zeitgeist

South and Central Americans
Koreans
Malays
Southwest Asians
Model minorities
Cultural identity
Cultural custom style
Family constituency
Responsibility
Existential/Person-centered theories
Collective unconscious
Reality therapy
Latino
Red
Individuality
Black English
Nature/people relationships
Edic
World view
Oppression/racism
Cognitive-behavioral theories
Archetypes
Rational Emotive

## KEY PEOPLE

C. Alexander
M. Arciniega
D. Atkinson
M. Bernal
S. Brown
K. Cella
G. Constantino
W. Cross
D. Dinkmeyer
P. Edmunds
H. Fishnaman
S. Freeman
P. Goldberg
L. Hansen
J. Helms

C. Arce
P. Arredondo
A. Beck
R. Blumenthall
M. Casas
L. Comas-Dias
G. Corey
M. Dillard
J. Draguns
P. Essandoh
W. Freed
E. Gama
B. Green
I. Helms
F. Ibrahim

## KEY PEOPLE (con't)

A. Ivey
S. Kagen
G. Knight
T. Lafromboise
C. Lee
D. Locke
K. Low
R. Malgady
R. McDavis
D. Meichenbaum
S. Minuchin
B. Newlon
T. Parham
P. Peterson
F. Perls
A. Psalti
L. Rogler
H. Sabnani
R. Sherman
D. W. Sue
T. Suzuki
R. Toporek
J. VanDusen
C.G. Wrenn

J. Jones
J. Klatz
W. Krogman
A. Lazarus
E. Levine
W. Lonner
M. Madsen
S. Martinson
S. Meggert
T. Midgette
G. Morten
B. Okun
P. Pederson
A. Pedilla
J. Ponterotto
C. Rogers
P. Rose
J. Sanchez
H. Stadler
D. Sue
R. Teske
J. Trimble
B. Wehrly
I. Yalom

## CLASSROOM EXERCISES TO ENHANCE INSTRUCTION AND STUDENT LEARNING

1. Divide the class into four groups and assign each group one of the four minority focus groups. Have each group prepare a listing of cultural/racial/ethnic factors that would need to be considered in providing counseling/therapy for this minority focus group. Have each group present its findings and compile a listing of similarities and differences between the four groups. Ask each group to translate the identified factors into counselor/therapist behaviors.

2. Divide the class into nine groups. The groups will correspond to the nine theories presented in the "counseling and therapy theories in terms of racial/ethnic components chart." Based upon its knowledge of the theory, have each group discuss what could be done within the theory to change the "O" (Theory doesn't address) to a "+" (Theory responds positively). Conduct a total group discussion so that all nine groups have an opportunity to share their recommendations.

3. Construct a panel of counselors/therapists representing the four minority focus groups. Have each panel member discuss his/her perceptions of the need for better understanding of multicultural counseling/therapy issues as these apply to the "real" world of counseling and therapy. Allow time for a question and answer period.

4. Construct a panel of former clients representing the four minority focus groups. Have each panel member discuss his/her perceptions of the importance of the counselor/therapist knowledge and application of multicultural counseling and therapy principles as these relate to the positive process in counseling and therapy. Allow time for a question and answer period.

5. Working in small groups (three or four members) have students review current professional and popular journals and periodicals for information pertaining to multicultural counseling and therapy. Have each group prepare an annotated bibliography of its findings with copies distributed to each student in the class. Allow time in the class for groups to discuss their findings. Follow each discussion with a question and answer period.


## INDIVIDUAL EXERCISES TO ENHANCE THE STUDENTS' LEARNING

1. Interview a counselor/therapist who works with clients from one or more of the four identified focus groups. During the interview, inquire as to what special knowledge and/or skills are needed to effectively deal with these client populations. Report your findings in either a written or oral report to the class. Ask your instructor for class time to share your findings.

2. Select one of the four minority focus groups of most interest to you and develop a paper or oral report dealing with some specific aspect of this group that has special application to your work as a counselor or therapist. You may want to select one of the areas identified in the chapter under "racial and ethnic cultural considerations." These include language, cultural identity, generation, cultural custom styles, geographical location and neighborhoods, family constituency, psychohistorical and religious traditions, and individuality. Ask your instructor for class time to share your findings.

3. Select one of the nine traditional theories critiqued in the "counseling and therapy theories in terms of racial and ethnic components chart" and present, in either written or oral form, a challenge to the authors' evaluation of the relevance of the theory to working with minority clients. Ask your instructor for class time to share your findings.

4. Review existing films and/or other audio-visual material that has application to the area of multicultural counseling. Critique what you find and ask your instructor for class time to either present your findings or to show or display one of the products

reviewed.

5. Based upon the information presented in the chapter and/or in the class, design what you feel would be an effective educational training program for counselors and therapists as this applies to multilcultural counseling and therapy. Ask your instructor for time to present your findings.

## QUESTIONS FOR STUDY AND DISCUSSION

1. What is meant by the term "culturally encapsulated counselor" and how does this term translate to the work of the counselor?

2. After reviewing the "counseling and therapy theories in terms of racial/ethnic components chart," what conclusions can you draw regarding existing theoretical systems and the issue of racial/ethnic applications?

3. What do you see as the factors that most impact the self-awareness of the counselor as these relate to racial/ethnic issues and what steps does the counselor/therapist need to take to assure that these factors do not negatively impact his/her working with the client?

4. What impact do such factors as "cultural identity," "language" and "cultural custom styles" have on counseling and therapeutic relationships?

5. What is meant by the following statement, "Counseling/therapeutic theories address the concept of mental health from the assumption of a universal (emic) Euro-American point of view to the exclusion of a culture-specific (edic) view?

## SUGGESTED READINGS

American Psychological Association (1993). Guidelines for providers of psychological services to ethnic, linguistic, and culturally diverse populations *American Psychologist*, 48(1), 45-48.

Arbona, C. (1990). Career counseling research and Hispanics: A review of the literature. *The Counseling Psychologist*, 18(2), 300-323.

Chan, C.S. (1989). Issues of identity development among Asian-American lesbians and gay men. *Journal of Counseling and Development*, 70(1), 16-20.

Cummings, J. (1986). Empowering minority students: A framework for intervention. *Harvard Educational Review*, 56(1), 19-36.

D'Andrea, M. (1992). The violence of our silence: Some thoughts about racism, counseling and development. *Guidepost*, 35(4), 31.

## SUGGESTED READINGS (con't)

D'Andrea, M., & Daniels, J. (1991). Exploring the different levels of multicultural counseling training in counselor education. *Journal of Counseling and Development*, 70(1), 78-85.

Davenport, D. S., & Yurich, J.M. (1991). Multicultural gender issues. *Journal of Counseling and Development*. 70(1), 64-71.

Fukuyama, M.A. (1990). Taking a universal approach to multicultural counseling. *Counselor Education and Supervision*, 30, 6-17.

Helms, J.E. (1984). Toward a theoretical explanation of the effects of race on counseling: A Black and White model. *The Counseling Psychologist*, 12(4), 153-165.

Huang, L. N. (1989). Southeast Asian refugee children and adolescents. In J.T. Gibbs & L.N. Huang (Eds.). *Children of color: Psychological interventions with minority children*. San Francisco: Jossey-Bass.

Lee, C.C., & Richardson, B.L. (Eds). (1991). *Multicultural issues in counseling: New approaches to diversity*. Alexandria, VA: American Counseling Association Press.

Locke, D.C. (1990). A not so provincial view of multicultural counseling. *Counselor Education and Supervision*, 30, 18-25.

Nwachuku, U.T., & Ivey, A.E. (1991). Culture-specific counseling: An alternative training model. *Journal of Counseling and Development*. 70, 106-111.

Pedersen, P. (1987). *Handbook of cross-cultural counseling and therapy*. New York: Praeger.

Skillings, J. H., & Dobbins, J.E. (1991). Racism as a disease: Etiology and treatment implications. *Journal of Counseling and Development*, 70(1) 206-212.

Smith, E. J. (1991). Ethnic identity development: Toward the development of a theory within the context of majority/minority status. *Journal of Counseling and Development*, 70(1) 181-188.

Vargas, L. A. & Koss-Chioino, J.D. (Eds.), (1992). *Working with culture: Psychotherapeutic interventions with ethnic minority children and adolescents*. *San Francisco:* Jossey-Bass.

## CHAPTER POST-INVENTORY

**INSTRUCTIONS:  PLEASE ANSWER THE FOLLOWING QUESTIONS NOW THAT YOU HAVE COMPLETED READING THIS CHAPTER:**

T    F    1.   The existence of **CULTURAL BIAS** in counseling and therapy has been documented by many authors.

T    F    2.   The history and legitimacy of **MULTICULTURAL COUNSELING** have paralleled the sociopolitical movements in the United States.

T    F    3.   Counseling and therapeutic theories address the concept of mental health from the assumption of a universal **(EDIC)** Euro-American point of view, to the exclusion of a cultural-specific **(EMIC)** view.

T    F    4.   **MINORITY** is defined as:  A group of people who, because of their physical or cultural characteristics, receive differential and unequal treatment due to collective discrimination.

T    F    5.   **WHITE CULTURE** is defined as the synthesis of ideas, values, and beliefs coalesced from descendants of white European ethnic groups in the United States.

T    F    6.   **ASIAN AMERICANS/PACIFIC ISLANDERS** represent the smallest minority group in the United States

T    F    7.   The importance of family is a major consideration for most **MINORITY GROUPS**.

T    F    8.   **STEREOTYPE** is defined as a flexible preconception about members of a particular group without regard for individual variation.

T    F    9.   **HISPANICS** constitute the nation's largest racial and ethnic minority group.

T    F    10.  **ETHNIC GROUPS** from different geographical locations exhibit distinct geocultural traditions and customs.

T    F    11.  **RATIONAL-EMOTIVE AND COGNITIVE-BEHAVIORAL THEORIES** challenge dependency, which to certain minority groups may be counterproductive to their concept of interdependency, an important part of their cultural values and one they view as essentially healthy.

T    F    12.  **EXISTENTIAL THEORY** is based on the understanding of the individual and allows the freedom to use other systems and techniques that can be made applicable to racial and ethnic groups.

**T    F**    13. By the year 2010, **WHITES** will represent 90% of the total population.

**T    F**    14. The term **NATIVE AMERICAN** is limited to only American Indians.

**T    F**    15. **ACCULTURATION** is composed of numerous dimensions, such as cultural values, ideologies, ethnic identity, beliefs, attitudes toward self, majority language use, cultural customs, practices, and ethnic perceptions.

**T    F**    16. **HISPANICS** comprise a large diverse group composed of Mexican Americans, Puerto Ricans, Cuban Americans, South and Central Americans, and others.

**T    F**    17. **AFRICAN AMERICANS** constitute the nation's second largest racial and ethnic minority group.

**T    F**    18. When working with **MINORITY CLIENTS** who still use their language of origin, understanding the language is not enough for the counseling/therapeutic practitioner.

**T    F**    19. For the minority groups presented in this chapter, the concept of **TIME** is very similar to the majority view in which the focus is the future; you sacrifice for tomorrow, and postpone gratification.

**T    F**    20. Counselors or therapists must be aware of the self-referent labels that clients choose. This is especially true for **MINORITY CLIENTS**.

# Chapter Eighteen
## _Counseling and Psychotherapy:  An Integrative Perspective_

**CHAPTER PRE-INVENTORY**

**INSTRUCTIONS: PLEASE ANSWER THE FOLLOWING QUESTIONS BEFORE YOU READ THIS CHAPTER.**

T     F     1.  Research has shown that **SOME THEORIES** are more effective than others.

T     F     2.  Theories are **DERIVED DEVELOPMENTALLY**, that is, each new theory incorporates some of the common knowledge of previous viewpoints.

T     F     3.  **AN INTEGRATIVE PERSPECTIVE** to counseling requires examination of one's beliefs, values, and personal characteristics, as well as theoretical constructs and tenets.

T     F     4.  Generally, **SINGLE-THEORY ADHERENTS** are more committed to and have a greater sense of ownership in their approach than do those who develop their own integrative perspectives.

T     F     5.  Compared to single-theory perspectives, **INTEGRATIVE APPROACHES** to counseling are potentially more flexible.

T     F     6.  As a rule, **NEOPHYTES** should avoid single-theory adherence because such a narrow perspective leads to a false sense of security.

T     F     7.  Dollard and Miller offer an example of how **MANY OF THE CONSTRUCTS** of two seemingly disparate theories, psychoanalytic and learning theories, can be similar in substance even though quite different in their use of terms.

T     F     8.  The **THERAPEUTIC ALLIANCE** between helper and client is unimportant in an integrative perspective to counseling because the flexibility inherent in this approach emphasizes outcome not process.

T     F     9.  Integrative therapists **SELECT STRATEGIES** and methods eclectically, depending on unique needs of their clients.

T     F     10.  Although integrative counselors **MAY BE ECLECTIC** in choosing methods, their role (helper, teacher, mentor, etc.) is invariant.

T     F     11.  Young's **REPLAN MODEL** of counseling is an example of a synthetic blend of two major theories.

T   F   12. Research suggests that **COMMON THERAPEUTIC FACTORS** may operate across theoretical boundaries and may explain why counselors from the same approach may achieve varying outcomes and why, conversely, counselors operating from differing approaches may be equally effective.

T   F   13. Prochaska's phase model of counseling is an example of **SYNTHETIC INTEGRATIONS.**

T   F   14. The **BASIC-ID MODEL** of Lazaras is a technical model of integrative counseling that is multi-model and broad spectrum both in terms of how clients' problems are conceptualized and how interventions are applied.

T   F   15. The **GOULDING'S REDECISION MODEL** of counseling is an example of the synthesis of two theories, Gestalt therapy and Transactional Analysis.

T   F   16. Research indicates that **SINGLE THEORY ADHERENCE** is more popular among practitioners than is adherence to integrative models.

T   F   17. Just about **ANY SET OF THEORIES** can be compatibly combined or integrated, even if their philosophical assumptions and beliefs differ.

T   F   18. Integrative approaches to counseling **HAVE BEEN CRITICIZED** for being haphazard and unsystematic.

T   F   19. Counselors who choose to be integrative in their approach to counseling experience **LESS OF A STRUGGLE** than do their counterparts who adhere to a single theory.

T   F   20. The **TREND AMONG PRACTITIONERS** is toward single-theory adherence over integration.

# CHAPTER 18 OUTLINE

**CHAPTER EIGHTEEN**
**Counseling and Psychotherapy: An Integrative Perspective**

I.    **INTEGRATIVE COUNSELING DEFINED**

II.   **HISTORY**

III.  **MAJOR CONSTRUCTS**

IV.   **INTEGRATIVE MODELS**
   A. Atheoretical Models
      1. Common Factors Models
      2. Phase Models
      3. Thorne's Model
      4. Bohart's Model
      5. Technical Models
      6. BASIC-ID Model
      7. Prescriptive Model
      8. Differential Therapeutics Model
   B. Synthetic (Systematic) Models
      1. Adaptive Counseling and Therapy (ACT)
      2. Interpersonal Style Model
      3. Redecision Model
      4. Strategic Model
      5. Actualizing Counseling and Psychotherapy

V.    **DEVELOPING AN INTEGRATIVE APPROACH**
   A. Philosophy
   B. Constructs
   C. Interventions

VI.   **STRENGTHS AND WEAKNESSES**
   A. Strengths
   B. Weaknesses

VII.  **CONCLUSION**

VIII. **REFERENCES**

## CHAPTER OVERVIEW

Since most counselors use some type of integrative model, this chapter is written to assist students in integrating information from various counseling approaches/theories into an integrative counseling model that best fits their needs and those of their clients. Following a brief introduction, this chapter defines integrative counseling and then describes its history and major constructs. Three integrative models are described: atheoretical models, technical models, and synthetic models. An important component of the chapter is the section on developing an integrative approach. Strengths and weaknesses of the integrative approach are carefully and objectively described. The chapter ends with conclusions and references.

## KEY TERMS

Atheoretical models
BASIC-ID
Common factor models
Conceptual synthesis
Core conditions of counseling
Counseling approach
Counseling knowledge bases
Counseling model
Counseling theory
Differential therapeutics model
Eclectic counseling
Eclecticism
Frey's model
Integration
Integrative approach
Integrative counseling
Systematic and appropriate use
Interpersonal style model
Lazy eclecticism
Metatheoretical model
Prescriptive model

Personal agenda
Personal model
Personal theory
Phase models
Professional integrity
Purist view
Rapport
Redecision model
Relationship
REPLAN model
Single-theory adherence
Stages of counseling
Strategic model
Strategies and methods
Synthetic models
Integrative perspective
Technical eclecticism
Technical models
Theoretical systems
Working alliance

## KEY PEOPLE

A. Allport
L. Beutler
A. Bohart
J. Brehm
S. Brehm
J. Clarkin
C. DiClemente
B. Duncan
S. Garfield
R. Goulding
R. Haven
K. Kelly
J. Norcross

M. Parks
J. Prochaska
G. Rusk
F. Thorne
M. Young
R. Diamond
W. Dryden
J. Frank
M. Goulding
J. Hart
A. Jones
A. Lazarus
J. Palmer

## CLASSROOM EXERCISES TO ENHANCE INSTRUCTION AND STUDENT LEARNING.

1.  Divide the class into groups of 4-6 students. Have volunteers assume the roles of helper, helpee, or observer and role-play a 10 minute counseling session. The talker (helpee) spontaneously stages and presents concerns. Helpers assume one of the following roles: patient listener (non-directive, accepting posture), problem-solving teacher (teach the talker how to define and solve their problems), didactic teacher (inform the talker what may be causing his/her concerns, suggest homework assignments, and coach him/her on how to change), mentor (role model how you, the helper, have faced and resolved similar problems), or investigator (use questions and other probes to help the talker uncover possible causes, historical and contextual, that may have lead up to their concerns and explore options for change). Rotate roles and role-play 10 minute sessions where you mix your role as the listener, teacher, mentor, or investigator. Discuss the following: Which roles felt most comfortable for you? Did you prefer a pure role approach or a mixed one? Which role(s) appeared most effective? How did the presenting concerns of the helpee pull the helper into various roles? Considering your values and beliefs, what helper roles feel most congruent for you?

2.  Theories develop from a common base of knowledge; yet, each theory is in some ways distinct. Divide up into groups of 4-6 and review the key terms at the end of each chapter. Classify terms, clustering those together that have similar meanings; for example, life plan in Adlerian theory and script in Transactional Analysis (TA). Form a list of unique terms, that is, constructs that appear in one and only one theory; for example, archetypes in Jungian Analytical theory. Form a second list of common constructs, noting the number of theories in which it appears. Have each group put their list on the board and compare them. Discuss any differences of interpretation.

3. The instructor will pass out old magazines, scissors, glue and butcher paper to groups of 2-3 students. Each group will be assigned a different theory, which should remain secret until the exercise is finished. Each group is to find pictures that depict their assigned theory, affixing them on the butcher paper with glue. After all groups have finished creating their collage, each shows it to the class. The class guesses which theory is depicted by the collage. Discuss which collages look most similar and most different, exploring how these visual presentations clarify similarities and contrasts among the theories. Cut each collage into fourths; now combine these fourths into various combinations to make a whole. Discuss how the integration of various theories appears when featured pictorially.

4. Technical eclecticism is a type of integration where the counselor uses techniques from a variety of approaches while remaining grounded in one theoretical base. Divide into groups of 4-6 and rotate being the helper, helpee, or observer. The helpee stages or role-plays a problem. Helpers attempt to help by using their preferred theoretical posture while borrowing eclectically from other theories in terms of techniques employed. An example of technical eclecticism would be operating from a person-centered theory base while using systematic desensitization to treat a fear. After you have rotated roles several times, use the material generated from your role-plays and discuss the following questions: Did using techniques from an approach different from your theory base feel awkward? Incongruent? Inconsistent? Do you believe the helpee detected any inconsistency? How comfortable are you in using techniques eclectically?

5. Divide into groups of 4-6 and brainstorm how theories are like other things, music for example. Which theory would you associate with classical music? Would jazz be an example of integrative counseling? Animals, cars, architecture, textures, sports, etc. may also be used in this exercise. Think of similes and metaphors you associate with different theories; share them with the class.

## INDIVIDUAL EXERCISES TO ENHANCE STUDENTS' LEARNING

1. As you learned earlier in this chapter, Beutler's model is based on persuasion theory (interpersonal influence). Using the following counselor-client interaction, explain how you would conceptualize this using Beutler's model.

   Counselor: It sounds like you are saying I just can't continue my marriage like this.

   Client: The pressures from my marriage are getting to me and are now creating problems at work. I'm tired of it all. No one understands what I am going through. None of it is my fault.

view and therefore do not respond to all counseling theories/approaches in the same way. Using the chart below, describe/predict how the racial/ethnic group might accept/reject the basic premises of the three models (atheoretical, technical, synthetic) of integrative counseling.

| | atheoretical | technical | synthetic |
|---|---|---|---|
| African American | | | |
| Asian American | | | |
| Mexican American | | | |
| Native American | | | |

3. Regardless of the theory, goals are an integral part of counseling. Yet unraveling the mystery around goals can be a simple two-step process as described below.

   **Step One:**

   Together the counselor and client list the client's major problems. Ask the client to select the most pressing problems to work on immediately (short-term goals). List the other problems to work on later as long-term goals. Assume the following problems were listed as major, immediate problem areas.
   - a. I am afraid I am going to fail out of college
   - b. I manage to find excuses/activities to keep me from studying.

   **Step Two:**

   With the client's help, take the client's problems (items 1 and 2 above) and turn them into goal statements with specific time dimensions.
   - a. Within four weeks, I will feel less fearful about failing out of college.
     Using the client example (exercise 1) write three goal statements.

4. In this chapter, the BASIC-ID was discussed as an approach to assessment and treatment. Each modality of the BASIC-ID is assessed and then an intervention is designed for each modality and implemented simultaneously. This approach has been labeled as a "shotgun approach" by Lazarus. Do you agree with Lazarus' statement? Be sure to be specific and thorough in your explanation.

5. In studying integrative therapy, students sometimes believe that they need help in differentiating the theories/models. To help you in aligning the theory/model with its basic premise, we have prepared Multitherapy Bingo.

# Integrative Bingo

Purpose:  To encourage the student(s) to become more aware of the differences between models/theories.

Type of Activity:  Individual or Group

Supplies:  Pencil, this book

Directions:  Put your name in the center box.  If you play this game alone (individual) then you should complete <u>all</u> bingo squares.  If you play this game with other students (group), then as with bingo, you complete a straight line or diagonal.  When you complete the line or diagonal, say "bingo."

# Integrative Counseling/Therapy Bingo
(set up in a grid, 5 across x 5 down)

1. Who was an early pioneer (1950s) of Integrative Therapy?

2. List the three major thrusts in Integrative Therapy.

3. The common factors model is an example of an atheoretical model. (True or False)

4. Name the six curative factors in the REPLAN.

5. Give three examples of atheoretical models.

6. Integration is a broad-based approach that makes systematic and appropriate use of the best interventions from all theories. (True or False)

7. Thorne's Model has been referred to as a medical model. (True or False)

8. The technical model is an undefined blend of interventions. (True or False)

9. The BASIC-ID model was developed by Lazarus. (True or False)

10. The BASIC-ID model is a good example of an atheoretical model. (True or False)

11. In BASIC-ID, to what do the seven letters refer?

12. Allport's model stresses technical integration instead of social persuasion theory. (True or False)

13. List your name.

14. The Redecision model mixes the conceptual framework and interventions of Gestalt and Adlerian. (True or False)

15. Redecision Therapy is an example of a therapy model developed by Goulding and Goulding. (True or False)

16. Name the three components of the Strategic model.

17. Most of the Integrative models are categorized under three models: atheoretical, technical, synthetic. (True or False)

18. Integration is the most common theoretical preference of counselors/therapists. (True or False)

19. A theory stressing that humankind is self-determining is psychoanalysis.  (True or False)

20. Theories <u>highly</u> focused on feelings include Reality Therapy and RET.  (True or False)

21. Theories focusing on action (not insight) include:  Gestalt, TA, and Reality Therapy.  (True or False)

22. Change in decision making is a major focus of TA, RET, and Reality Therapy.  (True or False)

23. All theories work equally well with all clients.  (True or False)

24. The ACA Ethics Code says that students in training must be exposed to a variety of theories.  (True or False)

25. The Counselor, whether in training or in practice, must abide by the ACA Ethical Code and always keep in mind that the welfare of the client is of paramount importance.  (True or False)

# Answers to Integrative Bingo

1. Dollard & Miller (1950) or Thorne
2. (a) helping client become aware of the problem situation
   (b) encouraging client to choose consciously
   (c) assisting client in developing a higher kind of personal integration through proactive choice
3. False
4. R = relationship
   E = efficacy and self esteem
   P = practicing new behaviors
   L = lowering or raising emotional arousal
   A = activating expectations of help and motivation
   N = new learning experiences and perceptions
5. common factors, phase model, Thorne's model
6. True
7. True
8. False
9. True
10. False
11. B = Behavior
    A = Affect
    S = Sensation
    I = Imagery
    C = Cognition
    I = Interpersonal
    D = Drugs or alcohol
12. False
13. Your name
14. False
15. True
16. (a) viewing the client's problem from various theory perspectives
    (b) choosing and applying the theory (theories) that best conceptualize the problem
    (c) Incorporate strategic interventions to enhance change
17. True
18. True
19. False
20. False
21. True
22. True
23. False
24. True
25. True

## QUESTIONS FOR STUDY AND DISCUSSION

1. Compare and contrast the merits of a single theory orientation with an integrative orientation.

2. Define eclecticism. How is an integrative theory different from an eclectic orientation?

3. Hackney (1992) states that there appears to be a convergence in theoretical integrity in counseling with humanistic theories containing some classical behavioral interventions, behavioral approaches acknowledging the legitimacy of feelings and affect, and systemic approaches using many cognitive interventions. Do you agree with Hackney? Describe some cross-theory interventions and their usage.

4. Discuss the major constructs in counseling integration.

5. What are the three types of integrative models? Define and give an example of each type of integrative model.

6. What are the steps involved in developing an integrative approach? Which do you consider to be the most important and why?

7. What are the major strengths of an integrative perspective? What are the major weaknesses.?

8. What theories would you use in creating your own integrative perspective? Defend your choice.


## SUGGESTED READINGS

Beutler, L.E., & Clarkin, J.F. (1990). *Systematic treatment selection: Towards targeted therapeutic interventions.* New York: Brunner/Mazel.

Garfield, S.L. (1980). *Psychotherapy: An eclectic approach.* New York: Wiley.

Hackney, H. (1992). *Differentiating between counseling theory and process.* Ann Arbor, MI: ERIC Clearinghouse on Counseling and Personnel Services.

McBride, M.C., & Martin, G.E. (1990). A framework for eclecticism: The importance of theory to mental health counseling. *Journal of Mental Health Counseling*, 12, 495-505.

Norcross, J.C. (Ed.) (1986). *Handbook of eclectic psychotherapy.* New York: Brunner/Mazel.

Patterson, C.H. (1989). Eclecticism in psychotherapy: Is integration possible? *Psychotherapy*, 26, 427-435.

Thorne, F.C. (1950). *Principles of personality counseling: An eclectic approach.* Brandon, VT: Clinical Psychology Publishing.

**SUGGESTED READINGS (con't)**

Watkins, C.E., & Watts, R.E. (1995). Psychotherapy survey research studies: Some consistent findings and integrative conclusions. *Psychotherapy in Private Practice,* 13, 49-68.

# CHAPTER POST-INVENTORY

**INSTRUCTIONS: PLEASE ANSWER THE FOLLOWING QUESTIONS NOW THAT YOU HAVE COMPLETED READING THIS CHAPTER.**

T    F    1. Research has shown that **SOME THEORIES** are more effective than others.

T    F    2. Theories are **DERIVED DEVELOPMENTALLY**, that is, each new theory incorporates some of the common knowledge of previous viewpoints.

T    F    3. **AN INTEGRATIVE PERSPECTIVE** to counseling requires examination of one's beliefs, values, and personal characteristics, as well as theoretical constructs and tenets.

T    F    4. Generally, **SINGLE-THEORY ADHERENTS** are more committed to and have a greater sense of ownership in their approach than do those who develop their own integrative perspectives.

T    F    5. Compared to single-theory perspectives, **INTEGRATIVE APPROACHES** to counseling are potentially more flexible.

T    F    6. As a rule, **NEOPHYTES** should avoid single-theory adherence because such a narrow perspective leads to a false sense of security.

T    F    7. Dollard and Miller offer an example of how **MANY OF THE CONSTRUCTS** of two seemingly disparate theories, psychoanalytic and learning theories, can be similar in substance even though quite different in their use of terms.

T    F    8. The **THERAPEUTIC ALLIANCE** between helper and client is unimportant in an integrative perspective to counseling because the flexibility inherent in this approach emphasizes outcome not process.

T    F    9. Integrative therapists **SELECT STRATEGIES** and methods eclectically, depending on unique needs of their clients.

T    F    10. Although integrative counselors **MAY BE ECLECTIC** in choosing methods, their role (helper, teacher, mentor, etc.) is invariant.

T    F    11. Young's **REPLAN MODEL** of counseling is an example of a synthetic blend of two major theories.

T    F    12. Research suggests that **COMMON THERAPEUTIC FACTORS** may operate across theoretical boundaries and may explain why counselors from the same approach may achieve varying outcomes and why, conversely, counselors operating from differing approaches may be equally effective.

**T F** 13. Prochaska's phase model of counseling is an example of **SYNTHETIC INTE-GRATIONS.**

**T F** 14. The **BASIC-ID MODEL** of Lazaras is a technical model of integrative counseling that is multi-model and broad spectrum both in terms of how clients' problems are conceptualized and how interventions are applied.

**T F** 15. The **GOULDING'S REDECISION MODEL** of counseling is an example of the synthesis of two theories, Gestalt therapy and Transactional Analysis.

**T F** 16. Research indicates that **SINGLE THEORY ADHERENCE** is more popular among practitioners than is adherence to integrative models.

**T F** 17. Just about **ANY SET OF THEORIES** can be compatibly combined or integrated, even if their philosophical assumptions and beliefs differ.

**T F** 18. Integrative approaches to counseling **HAVE BEEN CRITICIZED** for being haphazard and unsystematic.

**T F** 19. Counselors who choose to be integrative in their approach to counseling experience **LESS OF A STRUGGLE** than do their counterparts who adhere to a single theory.

**T F** 20. The **TREND AMONG PRACTITIONERS** is toward single-theory adherence over integration.

# NOTES

## ANSWERS TO PRE/POST INVENTORIES

| CHAPTER 1 | | CHAPTER 2 | | CHAPTER 3 | |
|---|---|---|---|---|---|
| 1. | T | 1. | T | 1. | T |
| 2. | T | 2. | F | 2. | T |
| 3. | F | 3. | T | 3. | T |
| 4. | T | 4. | T | 4. | F |
| 5. | F | 5. | F | 5. | T |
| 6. | F | 6. | F | 6. | T |
| 7. | T | 7. | T | 7. | T |
| 8. | T | 8. | F | 8. | F |
| 9. | F | 9. | T | 9. | F |
| 10. | T | 10. | T | 10. | T |
| 11. | F | 11. | T | 11. | F |
| 12. | T | 12. | T | 12. | F |
| 13. | T | 13. | T | 13. | F |
| 14. | T | 14. | F | 14. | T |
| 15. | F | 15. | T | 15. | F |
| 16. | T | 16. | T | 16. | T |
| 17. | T | 17. | F | 17. | F |
| 18. | F | 18. | F | 18. | T |
| 19. | T | 19. | T | 19. | T |
| 20. | T | 20. | T | 20. | T |

| CHAPTER 4 | | CHAPTER 5 | | CHAPTER 6 | |
|---|---|---|---|---|---|
| 1. | T | 1. | T | 1. | T |
| 2. | T | 2. | T | 2. | T |
| 3. | F | 3. | T | 3. | F |
| 4. | T | 4. | F | 4. | T |
| 5. | T | 5. | T | 5. | F |
| 6. | T | 6. | F | 6. | T |
| 7. | F | 7. | T | 7. | T |
| 8. | T | 8. | F | 8. | T |
| 9. | T | 9. | T | 9. | F |
| 10. | T | 10. | F | 10. | T |
| 11. | T | 11. | F | 11. | T |
| 12. | F | 12. | F | 12. | F |
| 13. | F | 13. | T | 13. | T |
| 14. | T | 14. | T | 14. | T |
| 15. | T | 15. | T | 15. | T |
| 16. | T | 16. | T | 16. | F |
| 17. | F | 17. | F | 17. | T |
| 18. | T | 18. | T | 18. | T |
| 19. | T | 19. | T | 19. | F |
| 20. | T | 20. | T | 20. | F |

| CHAPTER 7 | | CHAPTER 8 | | CHAPTER 9 | |
|-----|-----|-----|-----|-----|-----|
| 1. | T | 1. | T | 1. | F |
| 2. | T | 2. | T | 2. | T |
| 3. | F | 3. | F | 3. | T |
| 4. | F | 4. | T | 4. | T |
| 5. | T | 5. | F | 5. | F |
| 6. | T | 6. | T | 6. | F |
| 7. | T | 7. | F | 7. | T |
| 8. | F | 8. | T | 8. | F |
| 9. | F | 9. | T | 9. | T |
| 10. | F | 10. | T | 10. | T |
| 11. | T | 11. | F | 11. | T |
| 12. | F | 12. | F | 12. | F |
| 13. | T | 13. | F | 13. | T |
| 14. | T | 14. | T | 14. | T |
| 15. | F | 15. | T | 15. | F |
| 16. | T | 16. | T | 16. | F |
| 17. | F | 17. | F | 17. | T |
| 18. | F | 18. | T | 18. | T |
| 19. | T | 19. | F | 19. | F |
| 20. | T | 20. | F | 20. | F |

| CHAPTER 10 | | CHAPTER 11 | | CHAPTER 12 | |
|---|---|---|---|---|---|
| 1. | T | 1. | F | 1. | T |
| 2. | F | 2. | T | 2. | F |
| 3. | T | 3. | T | 3. | T |
| 4. | T | 4. | F | 4. | T |
| 5. | F | 5. | F | 5. | F |
| 6. | T | 6. | T | 6. | T |
| 7. | F | 7. | T | 7. | T |
| 8. | T | 8. | F | 8. | T |
| 9. | T | 9. | F | 9. | T |
| 10. | T | 10. | T | 10. | F |
| 11. | T | 11. | T | 11. | F |
| 12. | F | 12. | F | 12. | T |
| 13. | T | 13. | T | 13. | F |
| 14. | T | 14. | F | 14. | T |
| 15. | T | 15. | F | 15. | T |
| 16. | F | 16. | T | 16. | F |
| 17. | T | 17. | F | 17. | T |
| 18. | T | 18. | T | 18. | T |
| 19. | T | 19. | T | 19. | T |
| 20. | T | 20. | F | 20. | T |

| CHAPTER 13 | | CHAPTER 14 | | CHAPTER 15 | |
|---|---|---|---|---|---|
| 1. | F | 1. | T | 1. | T |
| 2. | T | 2. | T | 2. | T |
| 3. | T | 3. | F | 3. | F |
| 4. | F | 4. | T | 4. | T |
| 5. | T | 5. | F | 5. | F |
| 6. | F | 6. | F | 6. | T |
| 7. | F | 7. | T | 7. | T |
| 8. | T | 8. | T | 8. | F |
| 9. | F | 9. | F | 9. | T |
| 10. | T | 10. | T | 10. | T |
| 11. | F | 11. | F | 11. | F |
| 12. | T | 12. | T | 12. | T |
| 13. | T | 13. | T | 13. | T |
| 14. | F | 14. | T | 14. | F |
| 15. | F | 15. | F | 15. | T |
| 16. | F | 16. | T | 16. | T |
| 17. | T | 17. | T | 17. | T |
| 18. | F | 18. | F | 18. | T |
| 19. | F | 19. | T | 19. | F |
| 20. | T | 20. | T | 20. | F |

| CHAPTER 16 | | CHAPTER 17 | | CHAPTER 18 | |
|---|---|---|---|---|---|
| 1. | F | 1. | T | 1. | F |
| 2. | F | 2. | T | 2. | T |
| 3. | T | 3. | F | 3. | T |
| 4. | F | 4. | T | 4. | F |
| 5. | F | 5. | T | 5. | T |
| 6. | F | 6. | F | 6. | F |
| 7. | T | 7. | T | 7. | T |
| 8. | T | 8. | F | 8. | F |
| 9. | T | 9. | F | 9. | T |
| 10. | F | 10. | T | 10. | F |
| 11. | F | 11. | T | 11. | F |
| 12. | F | 12. | T | 12. | T |
| 13. | T | 13. | F | 13. | F |
| 14. | T | 14. | F | 14. | T |
| 15. | T | 15. | T | 15. | T |
| 16. | T | 16. | T | 16. | F |
| 17. | T | 17. | F | 17. | F |
| 18. | F | 18. | T | 18. | T |
| 19. | F | 19. | F | 19. | F |
| 20. | F | 20. | T | 20. | F |

# NOTES

# NOTES

# NOTES

# NOTES

# NOTES

# NOTES

# NOTES

# NOTES

# NOTES

# NOTES